16/8   CHR

"Michael Nicholas has produced a fascinating piece of work. This book will challenge you in many ways – particularly in how you make decisions in all parts of your life, not just in daily business. It takes the reader through a logical, data-rich and scientifically proven journey that will cause you to pause and reflect on numerous occasions. If you only read one book this year, I would highly recommend you make it this one – you will not be disappointed."
Stephen Murphy, President International Business, DJO Global

"I never normally get too excited about another decision making model or how to book, however this is an excellent read from Michael Nicholas. The book articulates as thorough a history and neuro-scientific explanation of decision-making through the ages of evolution as I have ever read, illustrated through great and at times tragically powerful examples and insights. It then concludes rather compellingly that the new way, despite the power of emerging artificial intelligence-based solutions, must nonetheless revolve around a human rather than machine outcome and contain a mindful approach at its core. I particularly loved 'The Inside-Out Challenge'."
Ben Bengougam, Senior Vice President Human Resources EMEA, Hilton

"Over the last few years, mindfulness has become part of the mainstream business dialogue. To have meaningful impact on performance though, we need it brought to life in such a way that it entices us to really change our thinking and behaviours, not dissimilar to the impact of a great school teacher on his or her pupils. Michael achieves this in his new book, creating a convincing argument that mindfulness can be a key driver in improving one of the most critical leadership capabilities – decision making. It is fresh, thought provoking and very stimulating. Definitely a book that I'll be recommending to others."
Robbie Feather, Commercial Director, Argos

"Rational decision making has long been the natural approach adopted by strategists and business leaders alike. But this book demonstrates that as the clock speed of business speeds up and business environments become more complex, this approach will become less and less reliable. Future business landscapes will place the emphasis onto learning how to develop aspects of mindset and judgment, rather than simply the empirical skills of old. Crucially, this book will show you how."
Rob Woodward, Chief Executive Officer, STV Group plc

"The word 'little' in the title of this book is deceiving. The book is jam-packed with thoughts and insights that will transform your understanding of decision making, demonstrating that there is a lot more to it than: doing it on a whim, with gut instinct or as some kind of knee-jerk reaction, but that a purely rational approach won't get you there either. Michael diligently covers the whole bandwidth – from learning from mistakes and breaking the rules, all the way to how mindfulness awareness can reshape decision-making abilities. Enjoy it!"
Kai Boschmann, Chief Marketing and Communications Officer, International SOS

"There can be no doubt that the number of decisions we are asked to make, and the amount of information available to consider in the process, are in exponential growth. So how can we synthesise and deal with such complexity quickly and confidently? This book will provide you with a completely new understanding of how to use your brain differently to make better and faster decisions. What's more, unlike many business books which I find to be quite turgid and uninspiring, this one manages to address a complex subject in depth, while remaining readable, digestible and stimulating. A brilliant book!"
Rhian Bartlett, Senior Director, Multinational eCommerce Corporation

"*The Little Black Book of Decision Making* teaches you how to train for success by dramatically improving your self-awareness, remaining in the moment, and focusing attention in a much more conscious and deliberate way. As I can attest from my own experience, as you do so you will become progressively more able to respond rather than reacting, enabling you to make decisions that are more flexible, creative, and appropriate to the challenges being faced. Like all things that are worthwhile, the application of the ideas in this book will require some effort, particularly at a mental level, but the results – including more consistent judgment and better relationships, both at work and in your life in general – will be well worth it."

Richard Crampton, Managing Director, Retail Trading & Services, Coop

"This book may surprise you if you have never looked in depth at the impact that our internal world can have on how we perceive and evaluate external events. It is one of the finest books that I've read dealing not only with the 'what' but also the 'how' of decision making, presenting a powerful case that improvements must start from within. This book will help you to do just that."

Aidan Neill, Chief Executive Officer, Bitposter

"Learn how you can develop to assure your success in today's ever changing environment... If you have read any of the many books on cognitive biases, but still found yourself wanting an answer to 'how' to improve your decision making, your interactions and ultimately your results, this book may be just what you have been waiting for. It draws on recent scientific discoveries to both explain why knowledge of these biases rarely allows them to be addressed effectively and what we can do to develop the mental capability and focus required. This is not a book that you can just expect to breeze through – it will force you to think. To me, that is a very good thing. I loved it. Michael is a true inspiration both as a coach and an author."

Michelle Burton, HR Director, Poundland

"If you want to progress beyond the standard, and well understood, approaches to decision making to which we have all become accustomed, to the highest levels necessary for leadership, read this book. It offers an in-depth explanation of why and when changes are necessary, and will show you how to turn that understanding into results that extend far beyond the norm."

Paul Sagoo, Chief Executive Officer, Lemon Group

"*The Little Black Book of Decision Making* provides a detailed exploration of the internal and external factors that drive decisions. Did you consider yourself to be a rational decision-maker? Read this book – it will give you pause for thought that definitely has the potential to improve your judgment. It shows how, by directing attention internally, towards our motivations and thoughts, we can increase self-awareness and thereby produce improvements in our external results. An engaging and insightful read."

Jat Sahota, Head of Commercial – Retail, Land Securities

"Michael offers a different level of insight as to why we make decisions in the way that we do, how the 'rules of the game' are changing and, more importantly, how we can improve our decision making. I doubt whether this is a book that you will want to breeze through in an evening, as taking the time for deeper reflection could deliver huge benefits in terms of your own self-awareness, the value of which is just one of the many principles that the book addresses. Great stuff, and it works!"

Darren Sinclair, Zone Managing Director, Sainsbury's

"Decisions are vital to the way we navigate our daily lives both within the workplace and outside of it. We make hundreds, perhaps thousands, of decisions of varying significance every day, and yet how many of us genuinely pause to think about how we can improve our decision-making and the underlying judgment that results in these decisions? Michael Nicholas' book challenges us all to think about what's at the heart of the decision-making process and understand how we can improve the quality of our decisions through mindful awareness of the role of the conscious and sub-conscious in our thought processes. Simply put, the key to good decision-making starts from the inside-out and being willing to understand, and change, ourselves."
Gareth Campbell, Senior Partner, International Consulting Firm

"This book is an incredibly enjoyable and thought-provoking read – exploring and developing an approach for attacking challenges that most of us are only just beginning to recognise or comprehend. Of course it is more than just a 'management' book for the workplace, with deep insights into thinking styles and emotional de-railers that can help outside of work too. In particular, it has reminded me of the vital importance of ensuring that I am always learning, while giving me the confidence to continue to grow and develop, and providing the direction to ensure that I do so efficiently."
Chris Green, Chief Executive Officer, Arcus

THE LITTLE BLACK BOOK
OF DECISION MAKING

THE LITTLE BLACK BOOK OF DECISION MAKING

MAKING COMPLEX DECISIONS WITH CONFIDENCE IN A FAST-MOVING WORLD

Michael Nicholas

CAPSTONE
A Wiley Brand

This edition first published 2017
© 2017 Michael Nicholas

Registered office
John Wiley & Sons Ltd, The Atrium, Southern Gate, Chichester, West Sussex, PO19 8SQ, United Kingdom

For details of our global editorial offices, for customer services and for information about how to apply for permission to reuse the copyright material in this book please see our website at www.wiley.com.

Wiley publishes in a variety of print and electronic formats and by print-on-demand. For more information about Wiley products, visit www.wiley.com.

Library of Congress Cataloging-in-Publication Data is available

A catalogue record for this book is available from the British Library.

ISBN 978-0-857-08702-7 (hbk) ISBN 978-0-857-08701-0 (ebk)
ISBN 978-0-857-08705-8 (ebk)

Cover Design: Wiley

Set in 10/12.5pt Rotis Sans Serif Std by Aptara Inc., New Delhi, India

Printed in Great Britain by TJ International Ltd, Padstow, Cornwall, UK

For my father, for always being there.

CONTENTS

ACKNOWLEDGEMENTS

Looking back over my 30-year career to this point, there are countless people who have contributed to my professional growth and development, and many more who have profoundly shaped my personal journey. Without them, I could not be doing what I do, living a life I love full of meaning and purpose. They include family and friends, my coaches, thought leaders I've had the opportunity to learn from, colleagues and clients. I have huge gratitude for them all.

I'd like to acknowledge several key teachers who have had a profound impact on my thinking and progress: Tony Robbins, for accelerating my personal development and awakening me to my own potential for transformation; John Maxwell for the many insights he provided about what it really means to be a leader; Daniel Goleman, who first got me thinking in new ways about how we can maximise relationships, influence and impact; Deepak Chopra for helping me to understand how our minds and bodies are interconnected, and for the huge impact he has had on giving my life meaning; Eckhart Tolle for deepening my understanding of the power of present moment awareness; Dr. Joe Dispenza for his insights into how we can evolve our brains, reshape behaviours and proactively transform our results; and my meditation teacher, Bhante Bodhidhamma, who inspires and helps me to become a more caring, compassionate and joyful person. Last but definitely not least, Sir John Whitmore, who sadly recently passed away. My introduction to coaching was with him around 20 years ago, and it literally changed the course of my life – without him, it is most unlikely that I'd ever have been in a position to write this book.

I'm also indebted to the publishing team at John Wiley & Sons. Without your encouragement, this book would never have become a reality. Particular thanks go to Annie Knight for her willingness to adjust the publishing schedule to match my writing speed, and to my editor, Pete Gaughan, for constantly challenging me towards higher standards.

A special thank you to my partner, Angela Howe Missen. You must have heard more about the trials involved in birthing this book than anyone should reasonably have had to bear, as well as having to accept the impact that it had on your life, yet you never wavered in your encouragement and support. This would have been so much more difficult without you.

And finally, huge gratitude for my family. Thank you to my parents, Ian and Marion, and my sisters, Sarah and Debbie, for your endless support. You mean the world to me. And finally, thank you to my two wonderful children, Amy and Hannah. You light up my life, provide a constant source of love, and inspire me to be the best version of myself that I can be.

ABOUT THE AUTHOR

Michael Nicholas has spent his career either as a leader him-self, or in helping other leaders to transform their impact, influ-ence, creativity and adaptability. He constantly challenges himself and others to question conventional wisdom and to revolutionise thinking and behaviour. With a track record of delivering results in multiple challenging environments, Michael understands and has learnt to manage the pressures his clients must handle to meet performance expectations in the face of uncertainty, time pres-sure and shifting goal posts. More importantly, he has a proven ability to convey what he's learnt to others. This enables the barri-ers to, and requirements for, high performance to be addressed at root cause, creating high-quality, lasting change and sustainable improvements in results.

Having started his training business in 2004, Michael has become a highly-experienced coach and award-winning professional speaker. He specialises in decision-making, emotional intelligence and employee engagement, with clients ranging from leading FTSE companies, through small and medium-sized enterprises, to dynamic entrepreneurial businesses. His insightful, results-oriented training is grounded in 30 years' of real-world experi-ence gained through working with leaders from a wide variety of industries, holding senior business positions, serving on active duty as a military officer, and completing the rigorous scientific training required to become a chartered engineer.

If you would like to find out more about Michael and his work, or to connect with him, you may do so at *www.michaelnicholas.com*.

INTRODUCTION

"As to methods there may be a million and then some, but princi-
ples are few. The man who grasps principles can successfully select
his own methods. The man who tries methods, ignoring principles,
is sure to have trouble."

—Ralph Waldo Emerson

Decisions are of considerable importance in practically every aspect of life. Professionally, they are arguably the thing that makes the difference to the level of success we achieve, because they determine how well every other talent or capability that we have can be applied. Our decision-making capability also determines the size and type of problem we can solve, and is therefore strongly related to how far we can progress and how much we will thrive.

There is no reason to think that the importance of decision making will reduce any time soon either. While I was writing this book, the World Economic Forum released its list of the top 10 skills they believe we will need in the workplace by 2020.[1] The top three were "complex problem solving", "critical thinking" and "creativity", all of which are vital elements of the mental capabilities necessary to make effective decisions (don't worry, if you don't recognise that creativity is a fundamental aspect of decision making, you will by the end of Part 1 of this book). Meanwhile, "judgment and decision making" was on the list explicitly at number six, and "cognitive flexibility", without which there can be no creativity, was in at number 10. So, the indicators are that if you want to be successful you'd better make sure you are a good decision maker. Let's take a quick look at what that might involve.

Although the decision itself occurs at a particular moment in time, to break down and understand the challenges involved we need to consider the whole process. This is a pretty standard approach:

1. Understand the problem.
2. Gather relevant information.
3. Analyse that information.
4. Draw implications from the results.
5. Identify options.
6. Decide which option to implement.
7. Take action.

Historically, experts have been sought out for their ability to go through this process quickly and reliably. Their previous experience would enable them to efficiently complete the first three tasks, because they would know what to look for. They would instinctively understand the implications of the data and be able to come up with range of scenarios for how to proceed without needing to go far beyond the bounds of what they had seen before, somewhere else. That is the nature of understanding "best practice", and it has been highly valued, for good reason. They would have a deep appreciation of how to implement the plan. Whether the skill involved was as a lawyer, engineer, scientist, medic, architect, consultant, entrepreneur or business leader, it has been pretty much essential, if we sought to progress, that we could demonstrate this decision-making capability. This was the route to recognition and respect, and a huge factor in determining a person's value in the marketplace.

Right now, we are at the leading edge of a transformation that will profoundly change all of that. I know, the term "transformation" is so overused, with many of the situations that it is supposed to describe, particularly corporate transformations, being little more than a bit of reinvention around the edges. Genuine transformation is what happens when a piece of paper is put in a fire – there is no going back. I use the word transformation deliberately, because there will be no going back from what is taking place right now. It has already started, and by the time it is over (to the degree it can be considered fully over), it will have fundamentally restructured the basis of how we, as human beings, will create value. The question is, will you keep up?

In 1987, as a junior officer in the Royal Air Force, responsible for the communications and navigation aids on an airbase, I had been updating our contingency plans for dealing with damage that might be caused by an enemy air attack. On completion of each section, it was sent to the typing pool; then, when it was returned, I'd proofread it for errors and send back any pages which had any so they could be re-typed. It was time-consuming, inefficient and pretty boring, but I didn't recognise that back then – I was just doing my job.

That was about the time I was offered my first computer, to which my response was, "What would I want that for?" I was relatively tech savvy having done a degree in engineering, with my final-year project involving writing computer code so that I could control part of a flexible manufacturing system, yet I still couldn't envisage how I could use a computer at work, much less how computing power might change the world of work (I'll be talking about this challenge to our decision making, which is called *bounded awareness*, later in the book). But lack of awareness in such circumstances doesn't shield us from the outcomes, and it wasn't long before all of us in that process, especially those typists, were forced to change.

Since then, while computing has revolutionised manufacturing processes and replaced many jobs in those industries with robots, for professionals and people in service industries, its impact has been relatively minor. Not many have lost their jobs, nor had to change the basic nature of what they do very much – they now just do it somewhat more quickly through a computer interface. Sure, we now have access to vastly more data at stage two in the process above, and we have computers to assist with stage three, but the underlying approach is the same, the way we think is the same, and so is our basic approach to adding value. But unless current forecasts are very wrong, this is all about to change in a way that will make what has happened so far look like little more than a ripple on the ocean, because artificial intelligence (AI) is coming, and soon, and with its arrival many jobs will go.

Just think what smart machines will do to decision making. Already, they can outperform experts in stages two and three of the decision process above, covering the two areas that have most enabled experts to differentiate themselves. They can learn more quickly and accurately, they don't run out of capacity, they have perfect recall, and the best of them can even outsmart us in critical thinking tasks, such as medical diagnoses. What's more, they aren't subject to the well-known biases that can affect human beings (some of which I'll introduce you to in this book). How long before even complex business problems are being diagnosed, and actions recommended, by a machine?

If that were the whole story, we'd be in big trouble. The reduction in our ability to add value would be all but inevitable – a question of when, not if. However, there are things that we are uniquely capable of doing; skills and capabilities which look as though they will be beyond machines for some time yet, perhaps indefinitely. These include our ability to understand novel concepts and situations, to connect with human beings at emotional levels, and to create, innovate and invent. We need to play to these strengths, and the interesting thing is that as the pace of change in the world increases, led by advanced technology such as AI systems, so does the demand for these human capabilities.

One area where this is especially true is in decision making, where success in meeting the needs and challenges of the new world will no longer be about the size of the problem you can handle, but more to do with the type of problem that you can solve. This is not just a response to smart machines – it is happening anyway, because of the volatility, uncertainty, complexity and ambiguity that have been such popular topics for leadership and business articles in general over the last few years. I'll show you in this book why the challenges created by a highly unpredictable environment can't be met with the form of decision making that uses a process like the one outlined above, and what you'll need to do instead. We'll look at some of the capabilities that will enable you to stay relevant and to continue to add value, whatever technology delivers.

What I hope to demonstrate is that your ability to perceive or think differently, which is within everyone's grasp, is going to be more important to decision making than any specific knowledge you may have gathered to date.

That's the good news. The bad news is that not many people have yet put much effort into developing the capabilities needed in this new world, or even know how to go about doing so. To be successful, you'll need a different focus to the one that you've been taught ever since you went to school, and which society has typically acknowledged and rewarded. You'll also need a different approach to the learning that is needed from that which we've always been taught. It's not really about "methods" or "techniques" – that approach would need an encyclopedia to cover all of the angles, and there would still be gaps. It is going to be about integrating a set of solid principles, based on sound understanding about how our minds and brains work, which can equip you both for what is happening and what is to come.

That is what I've sought to address in this book. Each chapter will introduce one principle, each of which I believe to be critical to developing the decision-making capabilities needed for the future. They are presented within a structured framework that will help you to gain a deep understanding of the relevance of each one. As this understanding grows, so you know what to do and why, the "how" that I'll describe in Part 3 will get easier.

I hope you will enjoy the book, find it interesting and that it will challenge some of your established beliefs, because that is how learning takes place. But even more than that, this is a time when knowing is not enough – we must take action – so I hope it will inspire you to do the personal work necessary to put the principles I'll be covering into practice. Know that if you do nothing, that is still a decision – it's a decision in favour of the status quo. It's a decision not to change. It's a decision to put comfort ahead of opportunity. And, as you will see, it's a decision that risks you waking up one day and realising that the world has changed and that you didn't take advantage of it. Or, alternatively, you could take the decision to get ahead of the curve, so that you will start to accrue benefits in advance and be ready when the full force of the coming transformation hits us.

Note

1. www.weforum.org/agenda/2016/01/the-10-skills-you-need-to-thrive-in-the-fourth-industrial-revolution/.

Part One

No Place for Old Dogs: New Tricks Required

LET'S GET REAL: WE ALL MAKE MISTAKES

At 11.38 a.m. on 28 January 1986, the NASA space shuttle *Challenger* took off from Kennedy Space Centre at Cape Canaveral, Florida. Seventy-three seconds later, as it broke up, the liquid hydrogen and oxygen that was by then streaming from its ruptured fuel tanks explosively caught fire and enveloped the rapidly disintegrating spacecraft. The deaths of its seven crew members – including Christa McAuliffe, who would have been the first teacher into space – in such a catastrophic and shockingly visible way may well be the reason why this disaster, despite it having no real impact on the lives of the vast majority of those observing it, became the third fastest spreading news story ever.

Following the accident, U.S. President Reagan rapidly set up a special commission (known as the Rogers Commission, after its chairman) to investigate it. The consensus of its members was that the disintegration of the vehicle began after the failure of a seal between two segments of the right solid rocket booster (SRB). Specifically, two rubber O-rings designed to prevent hot gases from leaking through the joint during the rocket motor's propellant burn failed due to cold temperatures on the morning of the launch. One of the commission's members, theoretical physicist Richard Feynman, even demonstrated during a televised hearing how the O-rings became less resilient and subject to failure at the temperatures that were experienced on the day by immersing a sample of the material in a glass of iced water. There is no evidence that any other component of the space shuttle contributed to the failure.

I've found, from years of asking participants in my decision-making workshops, that most people's memory of that day aligns with the summary in the paragraphs above. Though relatively few are aware of the precise name of the actual component involved, they consistently remember only the seal failure. This root cause appears unambiguous. So why would the Rogers Commission have concluded, as they did, that the key factors contributing to the accident were NASA's organisational culture and decision-making processes, not the technical fault? We need to take a deeper look.

First Appearances are Often Deceptive

Full details of the events leading up to the Challenger disaster are a matter of public record,[1] so I won't recount them in detail here. Bear in mind as you read the string of glaring errors below that this was the same organisation that achieved the incredible feat of landing men on the moon and returning them home safely, and which resolutely refused to succumb to the enormous challenges it faced in getting the stricken Apollo 13 crew back home safely when that mission suffered an oxygen tank explosion over two hundred thousand miles from Earth.

Let's return to that ill-fated Tuesday morning in January 1986. Several key facts shed light on the finding of the Rogers Commission that decision-making errors were at the heart of the catastrophe:

- The O-rings had not been designed for use at the unusually cold conditions of the morning of the launch, which was approximately -2°C. They had never been tested below 10°C, and there was no test data to indicate that they would be safe at those temperatures (which were around 14°C lower than the coldest previous launch).

• NASA managers had known for almost a decade, since 1977, that the design of the shuttle's SRB's joints contained a potentially catastrophic flaw. Engineers at the Marshall Space Flight Centre had written to the manufacturer on several occasions suggesting that the design was unacceptable, but the letters were not forwarded to Morton Thiokol, the contractor responsible for construction and maintenance of the SRBs.

• Engineers raised specific warnings about the dangers posed by the low temperatures right up to the morning of the launch, recommending a launch postponement; but their concerns did not reach senior decision makers. The night before the launch, Bob Ebeling, one of four engineers at Morton Thiokol who had tried to stop the launch, told his wife that Challenger would blow up.[2]

• In 1985, the problem with the joints was finally acknowledged to be so potentially catastrophic that work began on a redesign, yet even then there was no call for a suspension of shuttle flights. Launch constraints were issued and waived for six consecutive flights and Morton Thiokol persuaded NASA to declare the O-ring problem "closed".

• While the O-rings naturally attracted much attention, many other critical components on the aircraft had also never been tested at the low temperatures that existed on the morning of the flight. Quite simply, the space shuttle was not certified to operate in temperatures that low.

• It seems that one of the most important reasons why NASA staff opposed the delay may have been that the launch had already been delayed six times. Two of its managers have been quoted as saying, "I am appalled. I am appalled by your recommendation", and "My God, Thiokol, when do you want me to launch?"[3]

With this broader awareness it is easy to recognise that the technical, and obvious, "cause" of the accident – the O-ring failure – was really just an outcome of the complex structural problems arising from the relationships between the parties involved. Now, I expect that the Commission's conclusion seems completely unsurprising:

> *Failures in communication ... resulted in a decision to launch 51-L based on incomplete and sometimes misleading information, a conflict between engineering data and management judgments, and a NASA management structure that permitted the internal flight safety problems to bypass key Shuttle managers.*[4]

A report by the U.S. House Committee on Science and Technology went further. It agreed with the Rogers Commission on the technical causes of the accident, but was more specific about the contributing causes:

> *The Committee feels that the underlying problem which led to the Challenger accident was not poor communication or underlying procedures as implied by the Rogers Commission conclusion. Rather, the fundamental problem was poor technical decision-making over a period of several years by top NASA and contractor personnel, who failed to act decisively to solve the increasingly serious anomalies in the Solid Rocket Booster joints.*[5]

The Problem with Hindsight

In examining the events leading up to the Challenger accident, it would be completely understandable to have the urge to scratch your head and wonder how so many obviously intelligent people (we are talking about rocket science, after all) could have displayed such apparent ineptitude. How did NASA, an organisation that places such importance on safety, end up so flagrantly violating its own rules and appear to have so little regard for human life?

> *"Our comforting conviction that the world makes sense rests on a secure foundation: our almost unlimited ability to ignore our ignorance."*
>
> —Daniel Kahneman, Nobel Prize-winning Professor of Psychology and international best-selling author on judgment and decision making

When a decision has gone badly, the benefit of hindsight often makes the correct decision look as though it should have been blindingly obvious. But once you are aware of this bias, you'll see it everywhere – from the immediate aftermath of the horrendous terrorist atrocities in Paris in November 2015, where the press began questioning how intelligence services had failed to anticipate the attacks as soon as the "facts" leading up to them began to emerge, to football supporters who believe they have far greater expertise at picking the team than the manager, to the times when we second-guess our own decisions: "I should have known not to take that job", "I knew the housing market would collapse/go up", "I should have known that he was being unfaithful to me", "I knew that if I trusted her she'd hurt me", "I should have listened to my intuition", and on it goes ...

This "hindsight bias" refers to the tendency for uncertain outcomes to seem more likely once we know the outcome that has occurred. Because of it, we are prone to view what has already happened as relatively inevitable and obvious, not realising how the information about the outcome has affected us.

One of the first psychologists to investigate hindsight bias was Baruch Fischoff who, together with Ruth Beyth, used President Richard Nixon's historically important 1972 diplomatic visits to China and Russia as the focus for a study. Before the visits took place, participants were asked to assign probabilities to 15 possible outcomes, such as whether the U.S. would establish a diplomatic mission in Peking or establish a joint space programme with

Russia. Two weeks to six months after the visits had taken place, the same people were asked to recall what their earlier predictions had been. The results were clear. The majority of participants inflated their estimates for the outcomes that had occurred while remembering having assigned lower probabilities to those that had not. This bias also became stronger as the time between the initial prediction and the recall task increased. Many other events that captured public attention have since been studied, with similar results.

The heart of the problem seems to be that once we adopt a new understanding of the world, we immediately find it difficult to reconstruct past beliefs with any accuracy. This inevitably causes us to underestimate our own level of surprise at past events and, on the flip side of the coin, explains why it is so easy to be surprised when others overlook the obvious, as NASA did in the run-up to the Challenger accident.

Hindsight, because it is always 20:20, ensures that we feel on safe ground when criticising others' irrationality or lack of foresight; moreover, it simultaneously reduces our ability to evaluate past decisions objectively (our own or those of others). It can have an extremely detrimental impact on both decision making and decision makers:

- Decisions that don't work out can often be punished, because the variety of factors that were outside the control of the decision maker are difficult to recognise after the event.
- If decision makers come to expect that their decisions will be scrutinised with hindsight, they are much more likely to seek risk-averse and bureaucratic solutions.
- Irresponsible risk seekers can be undeservedly rewarded when their decisions work out because it is hard to recognise their gamble, so they don't get punished for taking too much

risk. Meanwhile, anyone who doubted them may get branded as conventional, over-cautious, or plain weak.

• Perhaps most importantly, hindsight severely reduces our ability to learn from past decisions. We'll look at why this is so important in the next couple of chapters.

We are all susceptible to hindsight bias, but it can be very difficult to recognise what is happening.

Running on Instinct

Psychologists use the term *heuristics* to describe the unconscious mental shortcuts that we take to arrive at judgments or solve problems. To date, dozens of them have been identified; hindsight bias being just one example. When we are faced with difficult questions, high complexity or ambiguity, or a need for high speed, heuristics can help us to find answers or solutions that would otherwise be beyond conscious reach. However, because they evolved to enable us to cope with an evolutionary past when we were living on the plains, hunting and gathering, the biases they introduce are often imperfect and may lead to terrible mistakes.

Mental shortcuts can even lead to inappropriate biases in life or death situations, as demonstrated by a study by Amos Tversky which looked at how the way that data is presented can affect doctors' choices. All of the participants received the same data on the effectiveness of two interventions for lung cancer: surgery and radiation treatment. It indicated that radiation offered a much better chance of survival in the short term, but a lower life expectancy over the next few years.

For half of the participants the data was presented in relation to survival rates, whilst for the others it was provided in terms of death rates; for example, the statistics for the surgical treatment of 100 patients were as follows:

Time Period	Survival Rate	Death Rate
Immediately	90	10
After 1 Year	68	32
After 5 Years	34	66

Clearly, from a mathematical/logical point of view, the two columns of data are exactly the same, yet 82% of the doctors presented with the survival data recommended surgery versus only 56% of those who were given the opposite perspective. Studies like this demonstrate the enormous influence that heuristics can have on our decision making; in particular, how difficult it is for us to divorce decisions from their emotional components.

Heuristics can be considered to be much like instincts. Animal instincts are easy to recognise; indeed, we assume that this is how animals do pretty much everything. As human beings, however, we generally prefer to think of ourselves as rational. We like to hang on to the evidence of our conscious experience, which suggests that our experience of the world is "accurate" and that we form beliefs and opinions based on the facts of the situation. Social psychologist Lee Ross called this conviction "naïve realism" – the conviction that we have the ability to experience events as they are. It enables us to justify any opinion as reasonable, because if it wasn't we wouldn't hold it! Sounds great, doesn't it? And it is completely wrong. The logic of this kind of thinking does not bear scrutiny, but that's okay because it's an easy choice not to investigate ...

Throughout this book I'll be encouraging you to take up this challenge: to investigate the activity of your mind and to make a habit of doing so. It is a vital element in making substantial improvements to your own decision-making capabilities. Let's start right now.

As you ponder the following questions, I'd like you to consider the idea that conscious awareness only provides access to the tip of the iceberg of what goes on in our mind, and that we have instinctive capabilities that go much deeper:

- When you see a breed of dog that you've never seen before, would you know that you are looking at a dog? If so, how? Check whether your descriptions could also apply to, for example, a cat or any other animal.
- When you see a caricature of someone you know well, would you recognise them? What gives you this capability?
- Would you be able to tell the difference between, say, a Scottish and an Irish accent (or any other two accents)? Just try for a moment to put a conscious description to the differences.
- If you walk into a room where two people have just been arguing, would you tend to be able to sense the tension in the room? When this happens, is it an instant feeling, or something that you have to think about? How can you tell?
- If you are like most people, you probably have little ability to describe the rules of grammar. So how is it that you, like almost everyone else, can probably use a wide range of these rules effectively most of the time in both speech and writing?

In each of these cases, and many others like them, the subtle distinctions that shape our awareness can be seen to occur automatically and virtually effortlessly. Almost any adult would readily recognise, for example, "dog" from "not-dog", even though any verbal explanation of how such a feat can be achieved would be highly incomplete.

The capacity to handle situations like those above stems from the enormous power of the unconscious mind, which can process rich and detailed information far beyond the limits of the conscious. Because of this unconscious capacity, we have the ability to solve many problems for which the conscious mind is completely unequipped. Even your capacity to read this text is enabled by your subconscious doing the hard work; hence, no thinking is required.

Accessing More of Our Potential

While heuristics are natural and automatic, awareness of them raises the questions:

- Could we learn to deliberately tap into this enormous unconscious capability in a more deliberate manner?
- Would doing so make a meaningful difference to our decision making?

The answer to the second of these questions is an emphatic "yes", which leaves us to address the critical question of how to achieve it. Doing so will require that you deliberately access a different type of learning to the one which has most likely dominated your professional development to date; one that trains the unconscious to do the heavy mental lifting.

When I was doing my officer training with the Royal Air Force, one of the other members of my team was an expert in aircraft recognition. Derek could somehow identify precise aircraft types from the tiny, fuzzy blobs in the photographs, and he was almost always right. But he couldn't explain how he knew!

Because enemy bombings could be significantly reduced by quickly and accurately identifying approaching aircraft, the same capability was highly valued in Britain during World War II. Several aircraft enthusiasts were found to be very good at this task, and efforts were soon started to enlist others. The problem was that, because there weren't many of them around, the only option was to train novices, but no matter how hard the "spotters" tried to explain their strategies, no one learnt to mimic their success. Like Derek, although the experts knew what they were looking at, they didn't know how they knew and therefore couldn't teach others what to do in the normal way. The information necessary to do so was not accessible to their conscious minds.

The solution was deceptively simple: trial and error combined with high quality feedback. The novices made guesses, and each time an expert would let them know whether they were correct. With each repetition, the novices' unconscous minds learnt just a little more until, eventually, they achieved mastery.[6]

It turns out that trial and error, with feedback, is the process by which we must learn to become proficient at any complex under-taking. We learnt to walk this way (with gravity and the floor as the feedback mechanism), to ride our bike (getting feedback from the corrective pressure of the hand on the back of the saddle, our stabilisers and, hopefully not too often, the ground), to read, play a musical instrument, touch type, or hit a tennis ball. Even activities such as running a meeting effectively or delivering a presentation require that the majority of the competencies involved are taken care of unconsciously. This is because the limited conscious mind is soon overwhelmed by the full burden of the various elements involved in even seemingly routine tasks.

In Chapter 8, I'll demonstrate that this type of learning is also vital if we are to make a non-linear improvement in our decision-making capabilities.

Great Power, but No Warning Bells

So we've seen that both heuristics and learned skills are essential to our capability to function effectively, particularly to achieve mastery. Each can come to feel effortless and natural, despite the complexity of the mental computations involved.

Because of the ease with which intuitive answers or solutions come to us, we feel confident of them, irrespective of their source. But when things that are hard seem easy, it is because a huge amount of brain capacity has been allocated to them, which results in an important paradox: *the times when we have access to our greatest mental capabilities are also the times when our ability to recognise any errors that occur is at its lowest.* This is because:

> We have no direct access to the mental processes of the unconscious mind, and ...
>
> both heuristics and learned intuitive responses are the preserve of the unconscious, so ...
>
> the more quickly we can do something, the more difficult it will be to recognise any errors that arise.

This feature of mental activity presents one of the most challenging obstacles to better decision making. Overcoming it will require that you learn to:

- consciously recognise the sorts of situations in which you are most likely to make cognitive errors
- slow yourself down enough to get yourself into an empowering mindset so that you can access the mental resources needed for effective decision making
- respond instead of reacting so that you can examine alternative perspectives and, hopefully, create new alternatives.

The bad news is that the times when you are going to need this capability the most will be those when it will be the most difficult for you to interrupt the way you normally do things. No mental "warning bell" will ring when you are running on automatic and on the brink of a serious error. This means that your progress is almost certain to be limited until you improve your ability to notice your own reactivity.

The good news is that it is quite possible to reduce reactivity and increase responsiveness – and if you do so you can be virtually assured that your decision making will improve. I'll explain in detail how to do this later in the book. Alongside that, if we can enhance awareness, so that you can observe events with what might be described as a higher level of "truth", perhaps we can even unlock the possibility of a non-linear change in your capability.

Multiple Levels of "Truth"

Picking up on that last sentence, you might be wondering how "truth" can vary. Our case study of the Challenger shuttle disaster and the subsequent discussion about how mental biases occur illustrates this point:

- Level 1: the disintegration of the spacecraft began following the failure of the O-rings in one of the joints of the right SRB. This is the most superficial explanation of how the accident happened – true, but also highly incomplete.
- Level 2: the O-rings would not have had the opportunity to fail had NASA's safety procedures been effective. The reason no solution was found was to do with the culture of the organisations involved, which resulted in years of poor

decision making. Since fixing this problem would have resolved the first as well, logically this must represent a higher-order conclusion.

- Level 3: a large number of intelligent and highly professional people made a string of incredibly poor decisions over an extended period of time. No doubt, the environment they were working in was extremely complicated, but it was also well understood by the experts involved. Nevertheless, as we saw above with the doctors choosing between life-saving treatments, emotions tend to trigger our human psychological biases and traps, this being the most fundamental explanation for the failures leading up to the disaster.

These three different explanations can be true at the same time because they hinge on perception. Thus, this example demonstrates the fundamental impact our minds can have when we are making decisions. It is quite obvious that solving the second-level problem would be of higher utility than solving the first because, having done so, Level 1 would take care of itself. Likewise, solving the Level 3 problem would be of more value than either of the other two, because by overcoming the psychological biases we would remove the root cause behind Levels 1 and 2.

Efforts to solve problems at too low a level, without getting to the primary factors involved, will tend to have limited results as, unfortunately, NASA highlighted through their lack of success in solving their problems post-Challenger. In the aftermath of the Columbia shuttle disaster in 2003, the investigation board that was set up to look into this accident concluded that "the causes of the institutional failure responsible for Challenger have not been fixed", and that "flawed decision-making" had resulted in this second accident as well.[7] Although NASA did make changes after Challenger, it appears that they were neither deep nor enduring enough.

The value in learning to perceive or think differently stems from the fact that this is the only way to solve new problems and thereby advance in life. We need a shift in awareness that brings potential new solutions into our consciousness. This is what I believe Einstein was referring to when he said: "We cannot solve a problem from the level of consciousness that created it." Perhaps NASA simply started at the wrong level.

In this chapter we've only scratched the surface of the many insights offered by the Challenger accident. Because of its depth, it has become a widely used case study into all manner of organisational issues, such as engineering safety, group decision-making, the ethics of whistle-blowing, and effective communications. However, important though the decision-making errors it highlights may be, the lessons that it provides fall far short of solving many of the most difficult challenges that are endemic in business today. There is another class of problem that has been gaining in importance since the end of the industrial age. During the last few decades we have been experiencing the emergence of a fundamentally different operating environment – one that dramatically increases the demands on decision makers. It is this shift, and its implications, that we must look at next.

Decision-Making Principle #1
We can access much more of our potential by learning to harness, in a deliberate way, the power of our unconscious mind.

Notes

1. For the full account on Wikipedia: https://en.m.wikipedia.org/wiki/Space_Shuttle_Challenger_disaster#Liftoff_and_initial_ascent.

2. This information did not emerge until 30 years after the event: www.npr.org/sections/thetwo-way/2016/01/28/464744781/30-years-after-disaster-challenger-engineer-still-blames-himself.

3. Howard Berkes, "Remembering Roger Boisjoly: He tried to stop Shuttle Challenger launch", 6 February 2012, www.npr.org/sections/thetwo-way/2012/02/06/146490064/remembering-roger-boisjoly-he-tried-to-stop-shuttle-challenger-launch.

4. Rogers Commission (6 June 1986), Report of the Presidential Commission on the Space Shuttle Challenger Accident, Chapter V: The Contributing Cause of The Accident.

5. U.S. House Committee on Science and Technology (29 October 1986), "Investigation of the Challenger Accident; Report of the Committee on Science and Technology, House of Representatives."

6. M. D. Allan, "Learning perceptual skills: The Sargeant system of recognition training" (1958) *Occupational Psychology*, 32: 245–252.

7. Columbia Accident Investigation Board (2003). Report of Columbia Accident Investigation Board, Vol. I, ch. 8, p. 195.

2

RULE MAKERS, RULE BREAKERS

"The history of life on this planet is a history of rule breakers. Life started ... as single-cell organisms, swimming for millions of years in the ocean, until one of those creatures decided, 'I'm going to do things differently today.' "

—Alejandro Sánchez Alvarado

Between A.D. 96 and 180 the Roman Empire was at its height, ruled by a sequence of exceptional leaders who have become known as the "Five Good Emperors". The last of them was Marcus Aurelius;[1] a man whose philosophy we know well because he left a record of his ideas in the form of a set of notes that he wrote to himself. The fact that these ideas are still in print with multiple publishers[2] is testament to the remarkable depth of his thinking. One of his insights was: "Look back over the past, with its changing empires that rose and fell, and you can foresee the future, too." To him, impermanence was the constant, though it is perhaps a little ironic that the decline of the Roman Empire would begin under the rule of his own son, Commodus, who succeeded him.

The man who first used the term the Five Good Emperors also had something to say on change. Niccolo Machiavelli is considered to be the father of modern political theory, and he observed:

"Whosoever desires constant success must change his conduct with the times." That was almost 500 years ago.

Clearly, the idea that change is inevitable, and that adaptation is therefore an ongoing requirement for success, is hardly new. But even a cursory look at most people's behaviours shows that recognition of this fact is still relatively rare. Let's consider a well-known saying that you may well be able to complete:

"If you always do what you've always done, you …"

For many years I've been asking workshop participants to finish this sentence. Without exception, the first response has always been something like, "… will always get what you've always got", or "… will get the same result". To most people this feels like a truism, but is it, in fact, true? If you carry on doing what you've always done, can you expect your results to remain unchanged?

I've asked the question countless times, and only three people have confidently and quickly answered "no". Almost every time, there is confident agreement that repeating past actions will continue to produce the outcomes they always have. However, as you already know from Chapter 1, the fact that something seems obvious is absolutely no guarantee of accuracy; it merely indicates that the reasons we believe it have been burned in the deeper, unconscious, recesses of our mind. As you'll see, that is certainly the case here.

A New Set of Rules

Until the 1600s, human beings in the Western world had a completely different understanding of how the world worked from that which is prevalent today. Before then, people had largely seen the world and everything in it as harmonious, interconnected and supportive. Disease and disaster were seen as punishment meted out by God, and angels and demons were accepted as invisible co-habitants of the world with us. Back then, no one bathed (unsurprisingly given that the doctors of the day advised that water opened the pores to infection!), and to the degree "laws" of nature existed, they were riddled with exceptions. Anyone seeking to understand "why?" in relation to any aspect of human existence had no alternative but blind acceptance of the answers offered by superstition.

Inevitably, in the absence of a solid foundation, decisions people made in those days were no more reliable than the superstition upon which they were based. However, all of that was about to change in a way that has had a seismic impact on the developed world. These days, we call it the Scientific Revolution, and it pro-foundly changed our beliefs about the universe and our place in it. Over a period of only 100 years or so, scientific theorems emerged that started to explain why things happen the way they do and, gradually, mathematical laws were developed that revealed that there was some order and predictability. Now, scientists saw the universe as being like a machine, made up of separate parts that behaved in foreseeable ways, making it possible to replace the unfathomable "why?", with a meaningful answer to "how?" The belief in a "clockwork universe" was born, certainty and precision became the new guiding principles, and the standard approach to decision making was radically revised – *to one based on predictability.*

As scientific thinking became more widespread, it was inevitable that someone would apply it to business, and that person was Frederick Winslow Taylor, an American inventor who is credited by many management theorists today as being the father of modern business management principles. By the end of the nineteenth century, advances in technological capabilities had catalysed the transformation of manufacturing processes; however, the overar-ching systems used to manage them remained largely unchanged.

Learning was unstructured and the expertise required to complete specific tasks was based on rules of thumb, where individual workers each developed their own approach based on their own personal experiences. The huge gap in thinking was that no one had thought to compare the effectiveness of the different methods, so everyone involved believed that their own technique was the best.

Taylor was a smart thinker. He had progressed rapidly in his career and, at the age of only 28, became the chief engineer at Midvale Steel. Because of his habit of regularly challenging the reasons behind people's decisions to do things in a specific way, he discovered that manufacturing decision making was governed by tradition, not rational thinking and sound principles. His solution? To start analysing everything: measuring what was going on, breaking every task down to its elements and timing each part. He assessed the efficiency of workers' actions and compared the different approaches, tweaking and tuning until he had found the fastest possible way to complete each step.

His results were nothing short of remarkable, increasing the speed of cutting steel in his factory from 9 feet per minute to 50, and all while using essentially the same equipment. It was such a mind-blowing transformation of capability that many people had to see it with their own eyes before they were willing to believe it.

Taylor's new approach represented the development of "best practice", enabling him to achieve productivity levels that would previously have been considered impossible. But this wasn't what earned him his place in the history books. That the impact of his success is still felt today is due to the innovation that enabled him to figure out what the transformation in his factory needed to look like:

He had developed a decision-making process *by which others could mimic his success in almost any field of business.*

With Taylor's breakthrough, the inconsistent artistry of individual workers, which had been haphazard and unstructured, could be replaced by the dependability of a scientific approach. The productivity gains this delivered were enormous and, unsurprisingly, his ideas were rapidly and widely adopted. The need for management expertise had been born.

Nothing New Stays New

"My team and I had worked hard to create a future for this company. Unfortunately, turnarounds don't always stay turned around forever."

—John Antioco, CEO, Blockbuster

In the late 1990s, when I was working as a strategist at Deloitte, a common challenge was to help clients to find ways in which they might be able to gain a strategic competitive advantage – ideally, to find an innovation with the potential to re-shape their industry. Back then, Blockbuster was one of the finest recent examples of a company that had achieved just that, having introduced a new business model that rapidly superseded the previous one and gaining a huge first-mover advantage in the process.

Blockbuster's creator was a computer programmer named David Cook. Motivated by need – his software business was suffering from a downturn in the oil and gas industry – he noticed that the video rental business was mostly run as a side-show within the core business of corner shops, newsagents and convenience stores, and that store owners at the time had no idea which films were in or out of stock. His innovation was to apply his knowledge of computers and databases to keep track of inventory, making him the only one who could optimise the selection of movies he offered based on demand. Then, he devised a store format that was both welcoming and family friendly, and Blockbuster had the formula that launched its growth.

From the opening of the first Blockbuster store, in Dallas in 1985, the next few years were phenomenal. In two years it expanded to become a regional chain of 19 stores and Cook sold the business to Waste Management for $18.5 million. By 1989 they were opening a new store every 17 hours, and in 1992 the company was sold to Viacom for $8.4 billion. Propelled by another huge innovation – revenue sharing with the movie studios – at its peak Blockbuster was a household name with a huge high street presence, having 60,000 employees in 9,100 stores, a billion customer visits a year, and a market capitalisation of $5 billion. Profits soared.

Then, in 2007, there was an even more rapid implosion. By 2010, just shy of 25 years after its launch, Blockbuster filed for bankruptcy. From zero to hero and back to zero in less than a quarter of a century!

What happened is becoming an increasingly common story. During the industrial age, and even into the information age, people leaving school could usually expect to stay with the company they joined for the duration of their working life – longer than Blockbuster was in existence. During this era, the lifespans of successful business models were typically measured in generations. New companies would be created, there would be a period where basic principles for value creation were worked out, then the model would be set into the corporate culture and delivered via systems and processes designed to ensure prolonged success.

Legend has it that in 1997, an unremarkable event occurred: a Blockbuster customer named Reed Hastings was charged $40 for the late return of "Apollo 13".[3] Blockbuster's late fees were highly profitable for the company, but much disliked by customers. But, unlike other customers, Reed Hastings didn't simply walk away dissatisfied – he created Netflix. From the start, he was was highly innovative:

- He wanted to get away from having employees and running shops, and so set up a model that used the post to distribute DVDs. A side-benefit was that it also removed the need for customers to drive to a store to rent or return videos, as they were forced to do with Blockbuster.
- Just a couple of years after launching the business, he overhauled the revenue model. He ditched payments each time a movie was hired and adopted instead a subscription-based model that allowed his customers to watch unlimited numbers of movies whenever they wanted, with no return dates or late fees.
- He was quick to realise that the future would be in online delivery, not physical discs sent through the post, and moved to video streaming at the earliest opportunity, redefining the industry for the second time in quick succession.

Where was Blockbuster's innovation during this period? Superficially, it certainly seems that Blockbuster, with its thousands of stores, might have become a bit of a dinosaur, unable to adapt to changing market dynamics and the rapid advance of new technologies, and that this created the opportunity for Netflix. But that isn't really the case. It wasn't easy for Neflix early on, and in 2000, with his losses mounting, Hastings tried to sell Netflix to Blockbuster for $50 million, suggesting that Netflix could become its online presence. Blockbuster dismissed the offer because it was pursuing its own strategy – with Netflix currently worth over $43 billion, how different the story might have been.

Even as late as the end of 2006, Netflix was in trouble. Blockbuster had launched a new DVD rental service called Blockbuster Total Access, which had 2.2 million subscribers, many of whom had switched from Netflix. At this point even Hastings admitted that they didn't know how to stop the rot and that Netflix was "in checkmate". No one could foresee what would happen next.

After a hostile takeover of the Board of Blockbuster in 2007, John Antioco, who had been CEO of Blockbuster for a decade, was forced out. His successor was a man named Jim Keyes; a retailer who didn't understand the basics of Blockbuster's business as a provider of entertainment. Keyes decided to pull the plug on the company's internet activities and to promote instead a vision of an "entertainment convenience store". He managed to snatch defeat from the jaws of victory. Within 90 days his strategies caused the entire leadership team to leave, and in the 18 months that followed he destroyed 85% of the company's value. By late 2010 the company began bankruptcy proceedings.

Clearly, at its core, this demise was nothing to do with the company being a dinosaur. Nor was it caused by Netflix. Blockbuster ultimately failed because its leaders were ill-equipped to handle the ambiguity and uncertainty of their environment, and to grasp what business they needed to be in as change took place around them.

Everything New Becomes Old

Blockbuster's legacy is not unusual: that of identifying a revolutionary approach to its market and implementing it successfully, but then failing to adapt sufficiently well to competitor activities and the next disruptive technology. Today – with the benefit of hindsight – it seems inevitable that a business model that required customers to drive to a store to rent a movie so they could watch it at home, only to have to repeat the process in reverse a day or two later (or suffer huge, profit-driving late fees) would become outmoded at some point. It looks equally obvious that a retail strategy would not work, and that more and more people would want flexible delivery of content to devices that may well be mobile, rather than have their viewing tethered to a single screen in a fixed location. But to suggest that these factors should have been equally obvious while they were happening ignores what we now know about hindsight, and is a huge oversimplification. If it were that simple, Blockbuster's story would a rarity but, in fact, it is becoming more and more common.

According to extensive research[4] by Boston Consulting Group (BCG), businesses are disappearing faster than ever before. Today they have a one in three chance of being delisted in the next five years, six times the rate of 40 years ago, and their average lifespan has almost halved (to just over 30 years). BCG's research has also found that volatility in revenue growth, revenue ranking and operating margins has more than doubled since the 1960s. And with 10 of history's 15 largest bankruptcies having occurred since 2001 it is clear that neither scale nor experience offers protection.

I expect that the problem with the old adage, "If you always do what you've always done, you'll always get what you always got" is now perfectly obvious. This statement can only ever be true under a very narrow set of conditions – that nothing else changes – yet even the largest companies and most successful of us can unconsciously fall foul of it. For example, IBM dominated the global computer market for three decades, but by the time Lou Gerstner took over as CEO in 1993 it only had 100 days' cash left. His explanation for how it had got there was as follows: "[IBM] got stuck because it fell victim to what I call the success syndrome. The more successful enterprises are, the more they tend to try to replicate, duplicate and codify what makes them great. And suddenly they're inward thinking. They're thinking, 'how can we continue to do what we've done in the past?', without understanding that what made them successful was to take risks, to change and adapt and to be responsive." Bill Gates said very much the same thing: "Success is a lousy teacher. It seduces smart people into thinking they can't lose."

That Reed Hastings was well aware of the problem of the "success syndrome" is clear from one of his blog posts, where he wrote: "My greatest fear at Netflix has been that we wouldn't make the leap from success in DVDs to success in streaming." He knew that he must change with the times to stay relevant. To cope with an uncertain future, we must all be courageous enough to leave the past behind. We must dare to be different. Because, as the quote at the opening of this chapter emphasises, no progress was ever made by following a set of rules. In fact, it is even worse than that: *if we always do what we've always done we are, in practical terms, going backwards.*

The Challenge of Change

So why are so many companies failing to respond effectively to changes in their markets? Why are market leaders falling like dominos, despite the huge resources at their disposal to plan their strategies? And what causes intelligent people to make seemingly obvious mistakes in such a predictable manner? It seems that the traditional approach to developing strategy is becoming less and less effective ... that something basic about their decision making must be flawed ... or perhaps that, for some reason, the implementation of new ideas must be difficult ...

Today, the default methodology used in most business decision making is still a direct consequence of Frederick Winslow Taylor's insights. Rational analysis, logic, business planning, problem solving and the like are so deeply embedded that they tend to be naturally assumed to be *the best approach* available. After all, they delivered, enabling businesses to achieve what would previously have been unimaginable levels of efficiency. However, once anything becomes automatic, assumed to be true – through a process that is normally known as *conditioning* – it also tends to become hard to notice when change would be beneficial, or perhaps even necessary. What if something important has changed, but not many people have noticed? In this world of scientific management, what if we should again take a look at the statement I made earlier, that decisions can be no more reliable than the superstition upon which they are based?

Okay, okay, before any scientists take offence (I'm glad to have your attention), let me say what I mean by this statement. Having started my career as a chartered electrical engineer, I'm not questioning the value of science. Merriam-Webster defines superstition as "a notion maintained despite evidence to the contrary". It is still true that decisions are still no more reliable than the beliefs upon which they are based, so what if those beliefs are wrong?

Recognising contradictory evidence is one of the biggest challenges we face in decision making, and I'll be covering it in detail in Chapter 4. Before then, in Chapter 3, I'll introduce some of the extensive evidence demonstrating why I believe there is a widespread over-reliance on rationality analysis, and explain why it is having such a negative overall impact on decision-making outcomes. First, we need to build on some of the discussion in Chapter 1 and take a deeper look at what is meant by *conditioning*, because psychologists tell us that it is the most basic and fundamental of our learning processes.

We are All Conditioned

You've probably heard of the infamous salivating dogs of the Russian scientist, Ivan Pavlov, which provided him with the first insights into how conditioning works. As part of his research looking at digestive systems, Pavlov was investigating the way that dogs salivated when fed. His discovery of conditioning originated from the chance observation that sometimes this salivation took place even when no food was in sight.

Pavlov figured out, through a series of experiments, that the dogs were actually reacting to the researchers' lab coats. What was happening was that when the dogs were served food, the person who brought it always wore a lab coat, and the repeated associations between the food and the coats had led to them becoming linked in the dogs' minds. Soon, the dogs began salivating on seeing the coats whether food was present or not. He then demonstrated that he could achieve the same effect by ringing a bell at feeding time. Quickly, the stimulus of the bell alone was enough to stimulate drooling. The dogs had been conditioned to unconsciously associate the sound of the bell with food, and this association then triggered the physiological reaction.

Here's a simple example of how we might learn a new conditioned reaction. Imagine that a young boy is bitten by a dog. This would be a traumatic experience for most of us, and it would therefore be unsurprising for him to think about it frequently. Each time he does so, he thinks of the dog and experiences fear, and before long he has a generalised fear of dogs which can be triggered by any dog, no matter how friendly. To make matters worse, his fear might then prompt a reaction that would increase the likelihood of him being bitten again in the future.

It is common in these sorts of situations to blame the original event, the bite, for the ongoing fear, but that is not how conditioning works. In fact:

It is his habitual thinking about the event, together with the failure to differentiate between different dogs, that is the real cause of the problem.

This is a critically important distinction that we will look at in detail in Chapter 5. We must think a thought repeatedly in order to condition it, the implication of which is that if we can learn to take charge of our thinking then we can develop the capability to consciously condition (or de-condition) ourselves in ways that will help to improve our performance.

Conditioning can also be passed from one person to another, such as through families. I shared one of my favourite examples of this phenomenon, involving a couple of newlyweds, in an earlier book, but I hope you'll agree that it's worth recounting here. As the husband was watching his wife preparing to bake a ham he was puzzled at why she cut the ends off prior to putting it in the oven. She told him: "Because that's the way my mother did it." Interested by this, he went to her mother for an explanation, but again was told: "Because that's the way my mother did it." Fascinated now, he sought out his wife's grandmother, who was by then quite old and fragile, and asked the same question; why did she cut off the ends of the ham? Her reply sums up the power that conditioning, and the unexplored assumptions that it tends to encapsulate, can hold over us: "Because we didn't have a baking pan large enough, so I cut the ends off to make it fit."

Interactions like this throughout our lives lead to us building up a myriad of beliefs and values. They may bear no relation to logic or truth, nor make sense in the current environment, yet they will still drive every aspect of our behaviours. Such beliefs and values will impact every area of our lives:

- The types of relationships that we desire.
- How we should conduct ourselves with others, particularly where there are national, cultural, racial, gender, generational or other differences between us.
- Our views about ourselves, such as our level of self-worth, beliefs about our intelligence, appearance, capabilities, weaknesses or any other aspect of our identity.
- What we consider to be "normal", or otherwise.

- The type of work that we want to do.
- How we enjoy spending our time.
- And, importantly, *our approach to decision making.*

Had we not been conditioned since birth, we would be almost continuously overwhelmed by life's challenges and completely unable to achieve mastery at anything. The process that I described in Chapter 1, whereby expert military aircraft spotters found they could teach others to mimic them, was actually a means by which the subconscious mind could be conditioned to do the work.

But conditioning has its downsides as well. Once we have established beliefs and well-practised patterns of behaviour, personal change at any level can become very difficult, and this is an important part of the reason why such a large gap often exists between what people know and what they do. It explains, for example, the strong tendency for people who feel extremely motivated having attended a training course, who are excited about making changes, to then fail to maintain their new behaviours over time. It's not that they didn't have serious intentions, but that they failed to condition the new behaviours, to make them automatic. Consequently, once they stop consciously choosing the new behaviour, they will naturally revert to their old conditioning.

Every person I've ever worked with already *knows* some things that they could do to improve their results, but knowing and doing involve different parts of the brain, and the understanding of how to create mental change at the level that is necessary is still quite rare. That you learn how to do so will be the key to you making significant improvements in your decision making as a result of reading this book, and this will be the focus of Part 3.

In order to prepare you for that, it is important for you understand more of the *what* and the *why*, so that you will know more and thus have more "know-how" in relation to your efforts to implement new behaviours. Simply put:

The more knowledge you have, the better prepared for a new experience you will be.

So, I hope that I've been able to demonstrate that conditioning is, in effect, the hidden force that drives our choices, that leads us to behave in a certain way in a particular situation. We have become "conditioned" once we have learnt to react automatically to a stimulus or trigger event, such that it results in ingrained actions and behaviours which involve little or no conscious thought. To make better decisions on a consistent basis, we need to learn how to condition our brains so that they literally operate differently.

Unexplored Assumptions

One of the downsides of conditioning is that, once the subconscious is in charge, any errors we make may be invisible to us, and one of the most important of them takes the form of an assumed constraint or limitation that then restricts us from accessing our full capabilities. Here, it is the recognition of the error that presents the biggest challenge.

A great example of this type of negative conditioning can be seen from the way that full-grown elephants can be restrained with just a light rope. This unlikely situation actually stems from when they are very young, at which time they were restrained with a similar rope – but at that age it was secure enough to hold them. By the time they have the strength to break free they have been conditioned to believe that they can't. They are imprisoned, albeit purely by their own minds.

The first person to identify and study this form of negative conditioning was Martin Seligman, a leading authority in the field of positive psychology. He ran experiments where dogs were first exposed to two types of stimulation – high pitched tones and brief, harmless shocks. As Pavlov had done with bells and food, the idea was to condition the dogs to feel fear on hearing the tone, so that they would react to it as they would to a shock. The dogs were then placed into a box with two compartments divided by a low wall. The intention was to teach the dogs to jump the partition in order to escape a shock, then to see if the same reaction could be provoked using the tone.

What Seligman hadn't anticipated was that the dogs made no attempt to get away when shocked. He realised that during the early stages of the experiment, when the dogs had continued to experience shocks irrespective of how they reacted, they had learnt that there was nothing they could do to avoid them. So, like the baby elephants learning that they couldn't break the rope that restrained them, the dogs also gave up trying.

Seligman named this psychological trait *learned helplessness*, and he went on to demonstrate its applicability to people. He discovered, for example, that depression is strongly associated with people having a sense of terminal discouragement underpinned by a belief that any action taken to solve their problems would be futile.

This kind of learned helplessness can have a dramatic and negative impact on decision making. At the heart of the problem lie unexplored assumptions – beliefs or ideas that seem true, that are accepted as certain, but which haven't been properly tested or proven. Such assumptions may:

- always have been false, but the realisation of this fact only came later; the world is flat
- at one time have been appropriate principles upon which to base decisions, but they have since been invalidated by

some sort of change of circumstances; there was once a lot of money to be made renting videos

• always have been false, but no one has realised yet. This is probably the most difficult category to recognise, as we will examine in further detail in Chapter 4.

Beliefs in these categories are often described as *limiting assumptions*, because they often introduce artificial constraints to decision making. Whenever we fall victim to them, they tend to close our mind to future changes of perspective, narrowing our sense of possibility, restricting creativity and reducing flexibility. They give us a comforting, but false, sense of safety and security; and even though an external observer with higher awareness might easily recognise our errors, the fact that the beliefs feel true to us can make it really tough for us to do the same thing.

Today, there doesn't seem to be much doubt that many of our habitual thought patterns are implanted in childhood; in fact, studies have found that babies are already making assumptions about the world by the time they are old enough to be tested. This process doesn't stop in childhood, however, and new beliefs can continue to emerge at any stage of life, either individually or within society as a whole.

In the context of this book, the combination of the deterministic science of the clockwork universe, together with Fredrick Winslow Taylor's scientific management, has shaped our beliefs about what constitutes high-quality decision making to an extraordinary degree. It might be anticipated that this type of rational thinking would have provided the tools to minimise the impact of conditioning, as well as its implicit limiting assumptions. In some areas that is probably the case. But there are three very big, and potentially dangerous, assumptions that arise as a direct consequence of our acceptance of this kind of deterministic approach to decision making, these being that:

1. Rational choice is a possibility for us.
2. Sufficient order or predictability exists for us to be able to apply a rational approach.
3. Applying a structured decision-making methodology will always lead to the best results.

All three of these assumptions will lead to sub-optimal outcomes at times. We'll begin to address the first of them now, and then cover points two and three, which are related, in the next chapter.

The Myth of Rationality

"We think, each of us, that we're much more rational than we are. And we think that we make our decisions because we have good reasons to make them. Even when it's the other way around. We believe in the reasons, because we've already made the decision."
—Daniel Kahneman

The assumption of rational choice is essentially the belief that when faced with alternatives, human beings have the ability to make a decision that stands the test of reason. And because this capability is highly valued, we have learnt to associate logic with intellectual strength and even personal qualities such as stability and honesty. Conversely, people lacking this rationality are often seen as indecisive, inconsistent, flaky or even mentally ill. It is not surprising that most of us like to be seen by others as rational.

Unfortunately, accumulating psychological evidence reveals that we are anything but rational, for example:

• When people place a bet on a horse, they feel much more confident that their horse will win just after placing the bet than just before.[5]

- The more often we are exposed to a stimulus, the more we will grow to like it (provided we didn't dislike it on first exposure).[6]
- We are much more likely to marry someone whose first name starts with the same letter as our own.[7]
- We are much more likely to agree with political initiatives by the party we support than exactly the same proposals presented from the other side.[8]
- As we saw earlier, doctors will make a different treatment recommendation depending on whether the effectiveness of the options is presented in terms of the chances of survival versus the likelihood of dying.

Neurological research continues to improve our understanding of why our behaviour can sometimes diverge so completely from the rational picture that we have of ourselves. It indicates that, when faced with decisions, we experience our feelings about a situation a split second before we can rationalise about it. This means that by the time we are thinking consciously, we are already being influenced by our emotions. Consequently, we might decide on a course of action that we know, rationally, makes no sense, but we make these poor choices nonetheless because of how they feel. For example, we might take that extra cookie when we are trying to lose weight, delay getting started on a project when we are already well aware that the timescales for completing it are inadequate, or get angry with a call centre operator at the bank because *we forgot* to pay our credit card bill on time and they refused to waive the fine. Here's another example: I'm pretty sure that almost all human beings get angry from time to time, but how rational is it to allow a discussion to get heated just because we don't like its direction? We all know that threatening behaviour never persuaded anyone to change their point of view! On the contrary, as we'll see in Chapter 4, it usually has the opposite effect.

So, we will be returning to this subject. For now, let me leave you with a suggestion which was beautifully expressed by David McRaney in his book, *You Are Not So Smart*:

The Misconception:

Your opinions are the result of years of rational, objective analysis.

The Truth:

Your opinions are the result of years of paying attention to information which confirmed what you believed while ignoring information which challenged your preconceived notions.

In summary, 300 years of scientific and management development have led to some major assumptions which are largely unexplored: assumptions relating to the universality of rationality, and that order and structure provide a consistently sound basis for decision making. Let's be clear, I'm not proposing that logic and rationalisation are bad – this approach has enabled us to solve lots of complicated problems. But I do wish to highlight that they have fostered an unconscious tendency for us to look for the "right way" to do anything and a lack of awareness of the inherent limitations of this approach.

If you want to improve your decision making, however, these limitations can't be ignored for much longer, because of the increasingly fast-moving and complex nature of the world we now live in. With more and more rule breakers, the game is changing. To help you to understand how this impacts you, we will look next at what happens when predictability starts to break down.

Decision-Making Principle #2
A prerequisite of making progress is that we leave the known behind, being willing to break some established "rules" about the way things happen.

Notes

1. The others were Nerva (96–98), Trajan (98–117), Hadrian (117–138) and Antoninus Pius (138–161).
2. In a small book called, *Meditations*.
3. Netflix tweet: "Happy Moon Landing Day!"
4. Boston Consulting Group, "The biology of corporate survival", February 2016.
5. Robert E. Knox and James A. Inkster, "Postdecision dissonance at post time" (1968) *Journal of Personality and Social Psychology*, 8: 319–323.
6. R. B. Zajonc, "The attitudinal effects of mere exposure" (1968) *Journal of Personality and Social Psychology*, 9: Monograph Suppl. no. 2, part 2.
7. John T. Jones, Brett W. Pelham, Mauricio Carvallo and Matthew C. Mirenberg, "How do I love thee? Let me count the Js: Implicit egotism and interpersonal attraction" (2004) *Journal of Personality and Social Psychology*, 87(5): 665–683.
8. Geoffrey L. Cohen, "Party over policy: The dominating impact of group influence on political beliefs" (2003) *Journal of Personality and Social Psychology*, 85: 808–822.

3

COPING WITH AN ERA OF ACCELERATION

"As far as the laws of mathematics refer to reality, they are not certain; and as far as they are certain, they do not refer to reality."
—Albert Einstein

In 2001, a little-known world record was smashed, changing in an instant the way people thought about their approach to the event in which it took place. For us, it provides a great illustration of how major breakthroughs in performance get enabled.

Prior to the event, it probably wouldn't have occurred to many people that the standard approach the competitors were using had been around a while, that the results they were getting with it had largely plateaued, and that the opportunity existed to do much, *much* better. What's more, it is easy, with awareness, to see this pattern all over the place:

- The cycle begins with someone developing a new and differentiating strategy or tactic.
- Next, inevitably, others seek first to catch up as quickly as possible through imitation.
- Everyone then attempts to find an edge by further refining the new approach with increasingly marginal improvements.
- The overall trend is gradually upwards, but no one stays ahead for long, as each gain they make is soon overtaken.

By this process, after a while, what was once fresh and different develops into "best practice", with an accompanying set of beliefs that become accepted as "conventional wisdom". Thus established, this belief system forms the basis of expertise in the area concerned and from that point, both consciously and unconsciously, guides decisions about the "best" or "right" way to approach the situation or event. Unfortunately, once experts start to believe that they know the answer, it also tends to introduce one or more major *limiting assumptions*, which block creativity and result in diminishing returns on effort and a levelling off of improvements. When this happens, the time is ripe for innovation.

At such times, real progress only comes from someone being willing to think differently – to break through the mental barrier that is limiting everyone else so that they can create something genuinely new. In the example I'm about to share, that someone was a virtually unknown 23-year-old Japanese man named Takaru Kobayashi, and the event was Nathan's Hot Dog Eating Contest.

Each year in this event, participants line up to see how many hot dogs (and buns) they can consume within a set time. Obviously, it's a bit of niche interest, but for those involved it's no joke, with structured training and mandatory licensing of competitors by the governing body, Major League Eating, and TV coverage that regularly attracts over a million viewers.

In the years leading up to 2001, the record had increased in relatively small increments, and at the start of that year's competition it was standing at 25 hot dogs in 12 minutes. During each round of the competition, signs are held up so that the crowd know how the competitors are doing. Kobayashi, in his rookie appearance, produced a total that was so large and unexpected that organisers ran out of pre-prepared signs and had to resort to writing them by hand. He smashed the previous record by eating a total of 50 hot dogs.

No doubt, this would have seemed impossible to most people until he proved them wrong by doing it! To do so, he simply redefined the problem. Whereas all of the other competitors were eating in the normal way, but more quickly, much as Winslow Taylor had done in his factory, Kobayashi optimised the action of eating for speed and efficiency. He separated the parts, breaking the sausage in half with one hand while dipping the bun in water with the other, placing them in his mouth one after the other and gyrating his entire body to encourage everything to lie compactly in his stomach. It was so radical, and effective, some of the other competitors stopped and watched.

Kobayashi himself went on to win for six consecutive years. He and others have continued to incrementally refine the approach, and today the record stands at an incredible 70 hot dogs consumed in 10 minutes, but still using the basic method that Kobayashi created. The *best practice* has now been well honed.

The Limitations of "Best Practice"

The mindset involved in much decision making today is comparable to that of the best hot dog eaters in the world just before Takaru Kobayashi turned up. The scientific management principles of Frederick Winslow Taylor have become embedded so firmly that their implicit assumption, of predictability and order, is largely unchallenged – with the result that "rational" thinking dominates, along with a tendency to see things in black-and-white terms. This is highly evident in strategic planning.

An aura of mystique has often surrounded the idea of strategy, but it is really just a plan of action for *how* things will get done to achieve some long-term aim. Normally approached with careful deliberation, as much information as possible is gathered to enable an understanding of things like historical patterns, the strengths and weaknesses of the current business model, competitor activity, and the direction and speed of potential technology advances. Then, this information is used to evaluate future scenarios and make predictions about what the environment might evolve to be like in one, three, five, 10, and maybe, in some industries (for example, nuclear waste management), even 50 or 100+ years. These projections then provide the basis for deciding what to do next.

At one time, this type of work was relatively easy. Henry Ford is famously remembered as saying:[1] "Any customer can have a car painted any color that he wants so long as it is black." But as the complexity of the environment has increased, so strategic work has become ever more challenging. Today, much of it relies on what has become known as "big data": data sets that are so large and complex that the first wave of computer-based data processing applications are no longer up to the job. Massive computational power and data storage warehouses are now dedicated to understanding who buys what, when and at what price. Every stone is being turned in attempts to link what consumers hear, read and view to what they will buy and consume under the assumption that this will lead to better decisions.

This is an approach to decision making founded in an *assumption of order*. It is an implicit expectation that with good situational analysis, by "getting the facts", then understanding the causal links between events in the past and using this knowledge to produce predictive models, we will be able to define "best practice" for the future – thereby finding the right or ideal way of doing things and enabling good decisions to be made. And so, every year, *big data* becomes bigger.

There is just one problem with this set of beliefs: *if there isn't enough order, it breaks down.* Best practice is, by definition, past practice, and it relies on predictability and the ability to iteratively refine an approach over time based on feedback. There is little room for the unexpected. Is this realistic?

Consider the fable of a monk who each day would predictably tread the same path across the town square. Becoming curious about what he was up to, the town's policeman stopped him to ask where he was going. The monk replied: "I don't know." Unhappy with this refusal to answer, the policeman asked again, but the monk only repeated, "I don't know".

You can probably appreciate the policeman's perspective – it is a stretch of normal logic to believe that the monk makes the same journey every day with no destination in mind …

So the policeman began to get angry and suspicious, demanding to be told where the monk was going and threatening to arrest him if he didn't tell him. But still the monk replied: "I don't know." With that the policeman arrested the monk and took him to the police station. When they got there, the monk looked at the policeman and said, "You see, I didn't know where I was going. I was planning to go to the market but instead I have ended up here. I really didn't know where I was going."

Though I first read this story many years ago, its power as a metaphor is increasingly relevant. Of course, the monk knew where he was intending to go, but that was not the question he was asked; he had enough awareness to recognise that if anything unexpected happened his plan might have to change. He constantly expected the unexpected and was comfortable living flexibly within this ambiguity.

At times your intention may bear little relationship to what you are actually able to achieve. However, I'm betting that you can achieve significantly more than you are doing currently, once you uncover some of the barriers that you don't yet recognise.

Blindsided!

When Takaru Kobayashi turned up and rewrote the record books, one of the most notable factors was the shocked amazement with which everyone else greeted his feat. Frederick Winslow Taylor created the same reaction when he increased factory speed: people had to see it with their own eyes before they would believe that what he'd achieved was possible. The same opportunity existed for everyone else, but they couldn't see it. They'd been blindsided.

We can all be blindsided, which often has a detrimental impact on our results. To make matters worse, there is an additional factor, which didn't exist in the examples of Kobayashi and Winslow Taylor, that can make us even more vulnerable. An example occurred when the almost unknown 21-year-old, Dick Fosbury, turned up to compete in the high jump at the 1968 Olympics and became the ultimate sporting flop. Over a period of just a few hours, he succeeded in establishing himself as one of the most influential athletes in history.

Advances in the high jump pre-Fosbury had progressed through the cycle outlined at the opening of this chapter. In the century to that point, three techniques had for a while been seen as best practice, but they all had a common element: they all allowed the jumper to land carefully, ideally on his or her feet. Fosbury's "Flop" was the first method to completely break the mould.

It is important to note here the importance of timing and opportunity. Until the 1960s, landing was done on relatively unforgiving sand, sawdust or low mats. Thus, athletes were forced by external conditions to land on their feet. Then there was an innovation – deep foam matting for landing on – and, fortunately for Dick Fosbury, his school quickly introduced it.

So, unlike the paradigm changes introduced by Kobayashi and Winslow Taylor, the Fosbury flop couldn't have happened earlier. But here's a critical question: once the new landing pits were available, why didn't every athlete create new jumping techniques? Why did almost everyone carry on doing what they had always done?[2] What blocked others from seeing the opportunity that was right in front of them? Why, when he was innovating in plain sight of his competitors though numerous competitions prior to the Olympics, did no one else think his approach might be worth a try?

Part of the answer to these questions comes down to an important characteristic of the human mind, and we'll be looking at it in detail in the next chapter. But there is also an element which is specific to Dick Fosbury and it relates to the fact that, prior to his success, he would have seemed an unlikely candidate for athletic stardom:

- At school, he liked sport, but had a self-professed lack of talent. Despite being 6 feet 4 inches tall, he couldn't even make it onto the basketball team.
- He tried several disciplines in athletics, and chose the high jump because it was the one in which he was the least useless. At 16, when he first attempted it, he didn't even reach the qualifying height for local club meetings.
- The technique of the day for the high jump was called the straddle, in which the leading leg is launched over the bar, with the body following face down. Using this technique, he couldn't compete – he hadn't even crossed 5 feet 3 inches, around 2 feet short of the world record.

- With two compressed vertebrae in his back (very likely a jumping-related injury), bad feet and a lack of physical strength, trying to work harder than the other competitors would have had only the tiniest chance of success.

No doubt, presented with these obstacles, lots of people would have told Fosbury not to bother trying – in their eyes he would have had no chance of success. But perhaps, on this occasion, that gulf between his level of capability and the proficiency of others actually played to his advantage.

"Necessity is the Mother of Invention"

It isn't clear who first used the proverb, "necessity is the mother of invention". Clearly the idea is old, but its psychological implications are still valid: once someone has no choice but to do something, they will think of a way of doing it. This certainly seems to have applied to Fosbury. Had the performance margin between him and other competitors been smaller, he might well have persevered with the straddle, but he was more than just hungry to improve and that made him opportunistic: *he had to innovate* to have any chance of competing.

On the other hand, for the other competitors, searching for incremental improvements to hone their already high levels of expertise would have felt like their best chance of success. They, therefore, wouldn't have been looking for anything radically new, and so they quite naturally missed the opportunity created by the new landing pits. They had their plan and, because of their focus on it, overlooked the fact that *the external environment changed*. The success syndrome in action again!

How often have you meticulously crafted a plan, only to have it become obsolete shortly afterwards because something occurred that changed the rules? Nothing can protect against this, as even the best-laid plan can become useless if something new happens. The question is, how often is that likely to occur, and to what degree is the assumption of order still valid in the current times?

Prepare for the Revolution

In Chapter 2, I cited research indicating that volatility in business is dramatically increasing. This is just the thin end of the wedge.

Professor Klaus Schwab, Founder and Executive Chairman of the World Economic Forum, provides compelling evidence[3] to support his conviction that we are at the beginning of what he has called the Fourth Industrial Revolution. The first used mechanical power to free us from reliance on animal and human effort; the second saw the advent of electrification and mass production, which allowed new social models and ways of working to emerge; and the third (often called the Information Age), by bringing computerisation and digital capabilities to billions of people, has enabled new ways of creating and sharing information that have speeded everything up and, in effect, shrunk the world.

Whatever we chose to call it (and others have used different terms), it seems likely that this Fourth Industrial Revolution will profoundly shift the way we live, work and relate to one another. It has already unleashed breakthroughs at a speed, and of a magnitude, that are unmatched by anything at any other time in human history, including:

- The *move from analogue to digital* technologies.
- A shift from old hierarchical structures to *a world run by networks*.
- An *explosion of choice* in virtually every aspect of life, which has shifted power from producers to consumers.

- An *acceleration in the pace of change* of virtually everything, driven by computers, the Internet, mobile phones and soon by commercially viable artificial intelligence.
- The development of a vibrant *global economy* in a way that is much more than just trade liberalisation and the globalisation of markets. While the Western capitalistic model has migrated East, in return, a new way of thinking and behaviour is becoming popular in the West, based on the East's more integrated, holistic and contextual models of the world.
- The emergence of *technological connectedness*: communication from anywhere to anywhere in real time.

It is hard to doubt that there is much more to come – this is big, and everyone seems to sense it. This fourth revolution is characterised by a transformational fusion of technologies that is blurring the lines between the physical, digital and biological worlds. No person, discipline, industry, economy or nation will be immune. It is even challenging our concepts of what it means to be human, as we grow our capabilities to alter the building blocks of life and to imagineer ever more capable artificial intelligence – smart machines which will take over millions of jobs.

Clearly, disruption on such a grand scale creates a huge potential for unanticipated changes. We now face a level of complexity, volatility, ambiguity and unpredictability in relation to future events which is unprecedented in human history. Inevitably, much of what is happening is unfamiliar, perhaps even threatening – and few of us are like the monk, comfortable to accept whatever direction life takes next.

This increase in complexity is happening not despite the advance of technology, but because of it. So perhaps it is not surprising that we should turn to the experts responsible for answers. Experts created this world, so why shouldn't we expect them to be able to answer the critical question posed by all of this change – the one at the heart of decision making:

What will happen next?

Experts and Chimpanzees

"For every complex problem there is an answer that is clear, simple and wrong."

—H. L. Mencken

I love the opening to an article on Wired.com by Johan Lehrer: "I often joke that every cable news show should be forced to display a disclaimer, streaming in a loop at the bottom of the screen. The disclaimer would read: 'These talking heads have been scientifically proven to not know what they are talking about. Their blather is for entertainment purposes only.'"

Like it or not, we are constantly subjected to a stream of projections about the future from financial advisors, TV pundits and innumerable experts and non-experts on everything from the stock market, to international relations, to the outcome of the next election. But is it as valueless as Lehrer suggests? Given that this kind of information provides the basis for so many decisions – when to buy or sell our house, where to invest our money, what we should or shouldn't eat, which team to bet on, which movie to spend our evening watching, and on and on ... if he's right, we have a problem.

The proof that Lehrer referred to comes from a huge study,[4] the most comprehensive of its type to date, by Professor Philip Tetlock of the University of Pennsylvania. He gathered together a big group of experts who made their living "commenting or offering advice on political and economic trends", to investigate their ability to make useful predictions about future events. He began by asking them to assess the probability of various things happening, such as: would there be a nonviolent end to apartheid in South Africa; would Gorbachev be ousted in a coup; and would the dotcom bubble burst. He also captured information about their thought process, so that he could better understand how they made up their minds. In all, over the 20-year period of the study, the experts made 82,361 forecasts, and as time passed Tetlock went back to check the accuracy of the predictions.

This piece of work has become quite famous, perhaps because the superficial conclusion that is commonly drawn from it is rather memorable: that the average expert "is not much better at predicting the future than a dart-throwing chimpanzee". Many of them, Tetlock found, would have done better if they had made random guesses. Even the best of them were consistently less accurate than even relatively simple statistical algorithms. Unfortunately, it looks as though Lehrer has a point.

What's the Problem with Complexity?

Clearly, if an environment is essentially random, trying to forecast with accuracy would be like trying to correctly guess the outcome of the toss of a coin. Fortunately, although the world we operate in is highly complex, it is not completely random. Could we not then expect to be able to develop the understanding necessary to cling to our familiar approach of using data and analysis to make predictions that worked so well in the industrial age?

The reason why the complex must be handled differently from the merely complicated started to gain traction with the publication, in 1948, of a paper by Warren Weaver.[5] He argued that "physical science before 1900 was largely concerned with two-variable problems of simplicity", but that this was not how the real world works. What was missing, he said, was the ability to deal with what he called *organised complexity*, where problem resolution requires handling "a sizable number of factors which are interrelated into an organic whole".

To illustrate this principle, Weaver used the metaphor of a billiards table. Classical science was good at analysing simple problems, he said, such as what happens as a single ball moves around the table. It could also handle the more complicated scenario of calculating the motion of two or three balls, though their potential to interact creates a huge increase in difficulty. However, introducing 10 or 15 balls creates a fundamentally different problem within which it very quickly becomes impossible to make predictions.

The exponential increase in complexity created by multiple interacting elements is extremely visible if we consider the number of potential positions that can occur on a chess board as a game progresses:[6]

- After each player has made one move, there are 400 different positions possible.
- Two moves apiece, and this number increases to around 72 thousand positions.
- From the third moves, more than 9 million outcomes are possible.
- Four moves each produce over 988 million possibilities.
- After only five moves, an incredible 85 billion permutations exist.
- It has been calculated that there are more conceivable chess games than there are atoms in the universe.

So even when we start with something that is apparently simple, if there are large numbers of variables we can see how quickly complexity explodes.

Unfortunately, hindsight, as we saw in Chapter 2, might trick us into believing that *big data* could one day get big enough to uphold its promise of perfect predictability, because after the event the factors that were important seem obvious. Given this bias, we'll naturally tend to believe that if we could just get that extra bit of critical data, we could do better next time. The desire for analysis can be seductive. That the reality is vastly different is far from widely recognised.

The problem is that when things get complex, data can only explain *how* things happened after the event and help us to create scenarios for what *might* happen next, and it does that only over the shortest of timescales. Taking this into account, it is easy to see why experts don't fare so well in the real world's complex interdependencies. Here are a couple of typical examples:

• Weather forecasts can be quite accurate over the next day or two (with occasional surprises), but as the uncertainties pile up and interact they are much less so just three or four days out. Beyond a week, predicting the weather is pretty much guesswork. Growing expertise, combined with more intricate models and the use of ever-greater computing power, is likely to enable some improvements in results, but there will always be a limit.
• In 2007, economists used 45,000 economic data series to estimate the likelihood of an impending economic meltdown. Their estimate of whether we would experience one as severe as that which actually occurred was less than one chance in 500, yet happen it did, and only one month later.

Science may still want to simplify everything into the simplistic model of the clockwork universe, but systems like these are just too complex to be tamed by analysis. At one level, I think we know this. For example, in snooker, when the best snooker players in the world break off, even though they would love to do the perfect shot, no one is surprised that the balls finish differently each time, because we know that tiny variations in starting set-up or cue ball direction will become magnified to create huge differences by the time the balls come to rest. Consequently, we have no expectation of being able to predict the outcome. Perhaps the same attitude would also be helpful in relation to economies, political elections, ecosystems and more.

The challenge is to make the awareness of the impact of complexity part of the way that you approach decision making. If you want to make more appropriate decisions, more often, it is critical to remember that:

> *If a problem is* complex, *hindsight never leads to foresight. In such an environment, rules built to handle the* complicated *are likely to reduce your decision making to the level of a dart-throwing chimp.*

Simple solutions won't address complicated problems, and complicated solutions are inadequate to address complexity. In the environment of the Fourth Industrial Revolution, you'll need to be able to recognise which of these contexts you are facing and to adjust your decision making accordingly. To help, in the following section I've summarised the key characteristics of each.[7]

Context Is Key

A *simple* system produces an environment within which facts are "known" and has the following characteristics:

- There is a strong relationship between cause and effect which is well understood.
- Systems and behaviours can be fully modelled, and the consequences of any course of action predicted with near certainty, making "right" answers self-evident.

- Like following a recipe to bake a cake, a formula can be followed and repeated with relatively little expertise and be expected to produce roughly uniform results.
- *Best practice* emerges.

Areas that don't experience much change and heavily process-oriented situations normally belong here, so decision making in this domain can be formulaic. In other words, KISS ("keep it simple, stupid") works. It is necessary only to be able to recognise patterns, as these then dictate the response or set of actions to be followed. This domain therefore requires little expertise and the approach that works is sometimes called recognition-primed decision making.

A *complicated* system produces an environment within which facts are "knowable" and has the following characteristics:

- Cause and effect are not immediately evident, but can be understood in general terms through analysis.
- Higher-order expertise is required, especially at the start, and a variety of fields may need to be drawn upon in order to produce a successful result.
- Answers involve trade-offs, and there may be many valid alternatives.
- Once a result is achieved, it will be largely replicable, though specific decisions still require further data analysis for outcomes to be predicted with confidence.

In this domain, there is still enough repeatability to allow theories to be tested many times over, in sufficiently similar circumstances that they can be shown to explain and predict outcomes. Because of this predictability, standard methods of decision analysis based on causality still work well. But they require expertise. You might be able to recognise a problem with your computer because it starts to slow down, but you'll need to take it to a technician to diagnose the problem.

A *complex* system produces an environment of "unknown unknowns" and has the following characteristics:

- The behaviour of each component is not explained by the properties of that component, but rather emerges from its interaction with all of the components (A will not always lead to B and on to C as it would in the complicated domain). This makes statistical analysis extremely difficult or impossible.
- Interactions are non-linear, so minor changes can produce disproportionately major consequences. Feedback continuously shapes the ongoing evolution.
- There are often tipping points, such as small events or thresholds crossed, which cause cascading effects which result in tremendous change across the system. Like trying to predict the start of a stock market crash, these tipping points are often difficult to anticipate.
- There is no longer a "right" answer, because solutions can't be imposed. Instead, they *emerge* over time as a consequence of the interaction of all of the elements of the system.
- Patterns appear which can, in retrospect, give the illusion of order and predictability, but constant change ensures that hindsight does not lead to foresight.

In this domain, it is necessary to plan more like the way that the emergency services do it. They cannot anticipate where the next civic unrest, road accident or fire will be. Therefore, they have had to build the capability to respond to the unanticipated as well as to any ordinary event. Netflix does essentially the same thing, focusing on recognising problems when they occur and fixing them quickly, rather than trying to predict every outcome ahead of time. When things are complex, adaptability, flexibility and "rapid recovery" are the names of the game.

At its extreme, *complexity* becomes *chaotic.* Here, the level of turbulence is such that cause and effect relationships cannot be seen even after the event. Like billiard balls, individual behaviours appear random, so this is called the realm of the "unknowables". Because of necessity, this is a great place for innovation!

Table 3.1 summarises how this model can be applied to three of the examples that I've already used in this book.

Even parenting can be categorised within this model. The young adult who has not yet had children will often have an idealised view of this task, believing that a set of solid principles will stand them in good stead (seeing it as a column 2 problem). But all children are unique, each one having many individual characteristics, so even the experience of raising one child provides no assurance of success with another one. Bringing up a child is actually a column 3 challenge.

It hardly seems surprising that few people have so far learnt to manage the challenge of navigating between these three domains effectively. The approach to decision making with which we have been conditioned may have proved effective in the world of cause and effect, but today it will leave you completely ill-equipped.

The Critical Differentiator

Think back to Dick Fosbury. His advantage clearly wasn't physical or material – he completely lacked any obvious sporting prowess. What set him apart was the same thing that enabled:

- David Cook to be the first to leverage the new technology of computer databases to differentiate Blockbuster, then the company to create a new economic model for the industry by revenue sharing with the film studios.
- Reed Hastings to take advantage of the compact robustness of DVDs, which enabled Netflix to send films by post, then to completely reinvent the company again with his adoption of streaming for video distribution.

Table 3.1. Examples of Simple, Complicated and Complex Situations[8]

Simple E.g. Production Lines	Complicated E.g. Space Shuttle	Complex E.g. Netflix
Optimised systems and processes are essential	Complex science and formulae are critical	Limited application of "rules" or "formulae" for success
Expertise is required during design phase only	Requires high expertise in multiple fields on ongoing basis	Expertise contributes, but is neither necessary nor sufficient
Characterised by repeatability	Extreme challenges handled via complicated body of expert knowledge	Principles of unpredictability must be embraced
Processes are easily replicated	Models can be developed and refined to become more accurate over time, reducing demand at the next stage	No "right" answer and one success does not improve likelihood of next innovation working
Results in standardisation	Produces set of critical principles for success	The business is unique, requiring individualised approach
"Best practice" produces good results every time	Likelihood of positive outcome increases as original issues resolved	Uncertainty is permanent

In each of these cases, the critical differentiator was, above all else, their *mindset.*

Because of their mindset, Kobayashi, Fosbury, Cook and Hastings were each able to recognise that the operating principles dominating their environment were just belief systems, not rules. This enabled them to be the first to take the opportunity to *rethink convention* and *redefine normal.* They applied their *creativity* to coming up with better solutions and *experimented* to make them work. Above all, the adaptability and creativity necessary to thrive in the complexity of the Fourth Industrial Revolution are determined and enabled by mindset.

Similarly, in the Tetlock study, what separated the experts who performed the best from those who were hopeless was their style of thinking. The most useful predictions came from those who were comfortable with complexity and uncertainty, and who also did not allow themselves to become overconfident (we'll talk more on why this is important right at the end, in Chapter 10). Once again, the differentiator was their mindset.

So, how can we equip ourselves with the necessary mindset? And how can we make sure of our ability to do so even when it is not entirely *necessary?* Those are big questions, and their answers will be the focus of the whole of the next section. But let me give away the punch line: paradoxically perhaps, to make effective decisions as things speed up in this age of accelerations, the most important thing we need to do is to learn to slow down. By the end of the book you will fully understand why.

> **Decision-Making Principle #3**
> As the pace of change increases, we'll face more and more "unknown unknowns", and that will place a new emphasis on the need for creativity in forward planning.

Notes

1. Henry Ford, *My Life and Work*, Doubleday, Page & Co., 1922.

2. There is evidence that a couple of other athletes were working on a similar technique, but they had not yet refined it to the point that they could use it competitively.

3. Klaus Schwab, *The Fourth Industrial Revolution*, World Economic Forum, 2016.

4. Philip Tetlock, *Expert Political Judgment: How Good Is It? How Can We Know?* Princeton University Press, 2005.

5. Warren Weaver, "Science and Complexity", published in *American Science*, 1948.

6. I am aware that there are some difference of opinion about the exact numbers, but there is complete agreement about the relative magnitudes at each stage.

7. Based on the work of Dave Snowden, the founder and chief scientific officer of Cognitive Edge, an international research network, which he named the Cynefin Framework.

8. Based on a model by Glouberman & Zimmerman, 2002.

Part Two

Mindset Matters! Getting Beyond the Process

4

WHAT COULD BE WRONG WITH "BEING RIGHT"?

"The greatest enemy of knowledge is not ignorance; it is the illusion of knowledge."

—Stephen Hawking

On the evening of 20 December 1954, a small group had gathered together in Dorothy Martin's front room. They were waiting for their midnight rescue by spaceship, ahead of the imminent apocalypse that Martin, their eccentric but earnest leader, had been warned would take place by dawn the next day.

This is one of the most famous doomsday predictions because a social psychologist named Leon Festinger, and two associates, were able to study the beliefs and actions of the "believers", both in the run-up to the event, and afterwards. After spotting a newspaper article about the group, the researchers decided to infiltrate them and to observe what happened when the prophecy failed.[1]

Martin claimed that she was getting her information from superior beings from the planet Clarion, who were communicating with her through automatic writing. They had warned her of the impending destruction, but promised that true believers would be rescued. Despite the obvious (at least, to most people) unlikelihood of the prophecy coming true, the researchers found that some of her followers were willing to go to extreme lengths to demonstrate their faith. Shunning publicity, many quit their jobs or gave away their homes, savings and possessions.

It is easy to imagine the scene as midnight passed without the arrival of the aliens. Initially, the little group tried to explain the non-event with the assumption that the clock must be wrong. But soon they began to get seriously worried. By 4 a.m., as they sat in silence, Martin began to cry. Then, at 4.45 a.m., Martin received another "message" saying that the group, "had spread so much light that God had saved the world from destruction". Despair turned to exhilaration, and the group that had previously avoided public scrutiny now actively sought to proclaim the miracle!

There could hardly be more tangible and inescapable evidence of a flawed belief than the failure of the world to end. Yet the believers in such doomsday prophecies consistently display the same trait – if they modify their belief systems at all, it is not by much, finding instead a "reasonable" explanation for what happened.

It is easy for us to mock such people, but actually, there is a warning embedded here for all of us: it turns out that we are all superbly skilled at explaining away even the most unlikely of contradictions when it is our own belief systems that are being challenged.

Who or What to Trust?

Imagine being a young parent, sincerely seeking to better understand how to help your children to stay healthy. You'd likely be very happy to find the article that CNN ran on 2 February 2011 entitled, *Germ Fighting Tips for a Healthy Baby*. It offered a long list of guidelines on how to prevent young children from encountering germs, the justification being that "[s]ince newborns have immature immune systems, every effort should be made to minimise their contact with bacteria and viruses that cause diseases". Nice, unambiguous and seemingly sensible advice with a clear course of action. You'd probably be quite happy, unless you read the article, *Why You Should Love Germs*, published just five months later on Parenting.com! It stated: "Overall, when it comes to germs, most people have it backward: with relatively few exceptions, they are good for our kids." Now what would you do?

Discernment over what to believe is critical to many decisions because this kind of conflicting advice is everywhere. Is emotional intelligence a game-changer or the latest fad? What is the best way to format your CV? How much fun should be allowed in the office? How much confidence is the right amount to display? What is the most effective way to exercise to optimise health? How much sleep should we aim for? Do cell phones cause brain cancer? Is no sun actually worse for our health than moderate amounts? Personally, I'd be happy just to know how much chocolate or red wine is actually good for me.

Sometimes, the advice we receive on such questions may be genuinely unbiased, in which case the problem is simply that vital information is either not known or has been overlooked. This leads to completely innocent, perhaps even unavoidable, errors. For example, many theories about the cause of illness, such as the miasma theory which held that we got sick from "bad air", were devised before we knew about germs. These universally look bizarre now. But think about this for a moment because it will become very important in Chapter 7: when you have no concept of germs, where would the first insight into the role of germs in disease come from? Doctors in those days were doing the best they could with what they knew.

Similarly, though I've tried hard to be as accurate as possible in this book, I'll be amazed if I've missed nothing, or if aspects of the contents don't get overtaken by our evolving understanding.

More difficult to handle than innocent errors stemming from a lack of awareness is the information which is presented with the deliberate intent to misinform or deceive. Unfortunately, there is overwhelming evidence that much "science" and "research" can be classed as misleading, exaggerated or completely false.[2] Here's what Dr Richard Horton, the current editor-in-chief of *The Lancet*, one of the most well respected peer-reviewed medical journals in the world, has said about it: "The case against science is straightforward: much of the scientific literature, perhaps half, may simply be untrue. Afflicted by studies with small sample sizes, tiny effects, invalid exploratory analyses, and flagrant conflicts of interest, together with an obsession for pursuing fashionable trends of dubious importance, science has taken a turn towards darkness."[3] Or there's this from Arnold Seymour Relman, editor-in-chief of the *New England Medical Journal*: "The medical profession is being bought by the pharmaceutical industry, not only in terms of the practice of medicine, but also in terms of teaching and research. The academic institutions of this country are allowing themselves to be the paid agents of the pharmaceutical industry. I think it's disgraceful."[4]

In 1944, for example, when the American Cancer Society said that "no definite evidence exists" to link smoking and lung cancer, perhaps they actually believed this to be true. But we now know for certain that the tobacco industry, governments and scientists continued to publicly deny this link for many years after the truth was known.

Even advice about decision making itself shows astonishing levels of inconsistency. For example, in the *Harvard Business Review*, a widely acknowledged source of very high quality information, there have been articles entitled *Don't Trust Your Gut*, *Learn to Trust Your Gut*, *Tell Your Gut to Please Shut Up*, *Intuition Isn't Just about Trusting Your Gut* and more. And this is just from one source! People who believe in the power of data say that we should use intuition as a last resort, only when driven to do so because of cognitive limitations. Others disagree, believing that there are times when gut feel produces better choices.

Pretty much wherever we look, we are faced with such conflicting, sometimes diametrically opposed, ideas. So what should we do? Rely on our own evaluations? That might not work quite as well as we would like to hope because, as I hope to demonstrate in the following sections, we are far too keen to trust what we already believe and we find it much more difficult to question our own hypotheses than might at first seem plausible.

Masters of Self-Deception

I suggested at the end of Chapter 2 that, while we may be comfortable with the idea that our beliefs are rational, logical and objective, this isn't generally true. Rather, most of the time we've done little more than to direct our attention to information that validates and reinforces our existing opinions while over-looking or ignoring any evidence that challenges our existing beliefs. To explore this idea, let's return to the doomsday believers, their seemingly unlimited ability to avoid recognising obvious flaws in their thinking and beliefs, and their consequent ability to hold onto their old belief systems almost unchanged even in the face of overwhelming evidence that they are wrong. It wouldn't be at all unusual if you need a lot more convincing that you too are susceptible to such enormous errors of judgment, would it?

It turns out there is a name for the psychological tendency that is at work in such situations: "cognitive dissonance". It refers to those times when there is a clash between different attitudes, beliefs or ideas which results in a state of internal tension. As this dissonance is unpleasant, the mind seeks to reduce the conflict between the two opposing thoughts, which is most easily achieved by altering one or the other of them. Cognitive dissonance has two dimensions:

- When there is a clash between an external idea or event and our internal model of the world.
- When an inner conflict exists between our own ideas.

Unfortunately, in the first of these cases, as I hope my example of Dorothy Martin's believers demonstrates, when the dissonance is generated externally, the easiest way to regain harmony is to reach for a new interpretation of whatever is creating the challenge. Whenever this happens, new ideas from outside are routinely dismissed. So powerful is this inner drive to reduce conflict, that things we value, such as truth and honesty, can easily take second place *without us even realising it*. And if we are capable of that level of self-deception in situations that are, to the external observer, so clear-cut, imagine how skilfully we can hang onto old beliefs when the evidence is ambiguous or contradictory.

The second dimension is inseparable from decision making because it is the inevitable result of the need to consider multiple ideas. For example, imagine that you have a choice between a new job which offers a significant career advance, or higher pay but less exciting medium- to long-term prospects with your existing employer. The new job will also involve a house move to a part of the country you love, but you'll have to leave your friends and family behind. Both alternatives have positives and negatives, so either way you will experience dissonance:

- If you stay where you are, you have a pretty good idea what you will get and the benefits of having more money to enjoy, but you also know that your career could level off. You get to remain close to your loved ones, but you'll miss out on that beautiful countryside.

• If you take the new role, your career prospects will be brighter and you'll have all the benefits of the new living environment, but there will be the disruption of the move, all the risks and uncertainty that go with it, less disposable income and you'll miss your loved ones.

Either way, once you make the decision, you close down the possibility of enjoying the advantages of the unchosen alternative, and get all of the disadvantages of the one you do choose. The mind doesn't like this, so to reduce this inner conflict it will interfere with your perception of the alternatives. This was the moral of Aesop's classic fable, "The Fox and the Grapes". The story is of a hungry fox that tries to eat some grapes hanging high up on the vine, but he can't reach them. Rather than admit defeat, he decides that he didn't really want them anyway, because they are probably either unripe or sour. This is where the expression "sour grapes", which is used to describe the envious disparagement of others, originated from. Clearly, people were having useful insights into cognitive dissonance over 3,000 years ago!

One of the first modern researchers of dissonance was Jack Brehm.[5] He used three groups of participants who were asked to rate several common household appliances. To say thanks for their efforts, two of the groups were given a choice between two of the products, the first group getting options that had very similar desirability, being only one point apart, and the second having options that were three points apart. The third group was simply given a product. This created much more dissonance for the first group than for either of the other two groups, because their choice between the products was much less clear-cut. Next, participants read reports on the various products and were asked to rate them again. This time, participants increased their rating of the item they chose, and lowered their rating of the rejected item – a clear (unconscious) attempt to reduce dissonance by increasing their perception of the attractiveness of the chosen alternative and decreasing the attractiveness of the unchosen alternative. Furthermore, those in the high dissonance group spread apart their scores by significantly more than either of the other groups because they had to go to greater lengths to reduce their internal discomfort. Now, perhaps, the extreme and seemingly counterintuitive reaction of the doomsday "believers", who went seeking publicity, makes sense – the more severe the dissonance, the more extreme the measures that will be needed to counter it.

The moral of Aesop's fable seems clear, that "any fool can despise what he cannot get", but, like when we looked at the "cause" of the Challenger disaster, there must be a deeper level of truth at work here as well, because people who are not fools readily fall into this mental trap as well. By understanding cognitive dissonance it becomes evident why people so frequently choose to criticise something that, in their heart, they might desperately want to possess, such as good looks, sporting or other prowess, financial or career success, intelligence, social acumen, etc. It also explains why we regularly see decent people, even in the face of the clearest inconsistencies in their position, resolutely justifying and standing by dishonest friends, disgraced politicians, discredited ideologies and disastrous decisions of all descriptions.

That these behaviours don't appear rational is not surprising, because they aren't. However, I hope you are starting to recognise one of the key aspects of awareness that will help you to improve your decision making:

There is a predictability to our irrationality.

This predictability increases as we better understand the impact of emotions (and the more we let go of the illusion of rationality).

There's No Avoiding Emotions

"The test of a first-rate intelligence is the ability to hold two opposed ideas in mind at the same time and still retain the ability to function."

—F. Scott Fitzgerald

Brain research is beginning to provide further insights that help explain what lies behind cognitive dissonance. For example, a study led by Drew Westen,[6] Professor of Psychology and Psychiatry at Emory University in Atlanta, Georgia, used functional magnetic resonance imaging (fMRI) to show that when we try to process information that creates dissonance (because it is inconsistent with our beliefs), *the reasoning parts of the brain virtually shut down.* This explains something that you are probably already well aware of: that it is harder to "think straight" when we are upset. In workshops, I often teach that *negative emotions make smart people stupid*, and this is an important part of the neurological basis for that statement (the other element is the fight-or-flight response that we'll be looking at in the next chapter). Dissonance creates discomfort, and thus maintaining a state of rationality is a very difficult thing to do (actually, this is not something that we can "do" at all, but we'll need to return to that point later, in Chapter 9).

Drew Westen also found that our emotional circuits are highly active when we are faced with dissonant ideas. When put together with the observation that reasoning circuits are largely inactive, this provides a clear indication that emotions are actually driving our decisions at such times. Furthermore, he also discovered that the reward circuits light up once the conflict has been removed. This is incredibly significant. These circuits are powerful motivators of behaviour: they are the same ones that become overactive when people suffer the cravings of addictions, which make it almost impossible for them to resist the urges to indulge in their habit. So, what this finding suggests is that the removal of dissonance is enough to enable us to feel good, and that the brain doesn't really care how we achieve it!

The technical term for this characteristic of our minds, where emotions drive judgment at a level below conscious awareness, is "motivated reasoning". Its effect on decision making can be catastrophic, because the resulting unconscious brain activity will tend to move us towards judgments that maximise positive feelings and minimise negative ones irrespective of the rationality of the decision – our brain would rather be happy than "right" and it's a master at hiding this from us. As a result, we find it easier to believe ideas that we would like to be true than those we don't like the sound of. In other words:

> *Much of what we call reasoning isn't really reasoning at all in the normal sense, because it is driven by emotional factors that are beyond the reach of conscious introspection.*

Clearly, this isn't good news for anyone who likes the idea that we are essentially rational creatures. Indeed, if this applies you, you might well be experiencing some of your own *cognitive dissonance* right now, created by the conflict between two ideas: your comfortable misconception that your opinions are the result of years of rational, objective analysis and the modern understanding that, actually, you are rather emotionally driven, whether you realise it or not!

I'm Right Because I Believe I Am

When faced with contradictory evidence, the desire to side with what is most comfortable – *cognitive dissonance* – and to avoid ideas that are contrary to what we believe – *motivated reasoning* – produces a very strong tendency for us to do little more than to seek to confirm our existing beliefs. This is the basis of one of our most powerful mental biases. If I had to identify one aspect of our mental processes that deserves particular attention because of its potential to lead to errors, over half a century of research has shown that this one would have to be a prime candidate. The name given to it is "confirmation bias", and it is inseparable from cognitive dissonance and motivated reasoning.

Confirmation bias refers to the tendency of decision makers to actively seek out and assign more weight to evidence that confirms some pre-existing expectation or hypothesis or that justifies their decisions, while at the same time ignoring or underweighting information that could disconfirm their ideas. Its purpose is to frame the world so it makes sense to us, but the price we pay is that we find it easier to believe propositions that we would like to be true than those we would prefer to be false. As a result, we will very often be wrong while at the same time being completely oblivious of this fact.

There are three ways in which our confirmation bias can distort even the best decision-making process:

- Selection bias: It biases choices about what evidence is relevant, restricting the information that gets selected for evaluation.
- Interpretation bias: It leads to a biased interpretation of the information that does get selected.
- Hindsight bias: It distorts our memory.

To examine the *selection bias*, researchers from Ohio State University secretly recorded how long participants spent reading articles in an online forum.[7] The articles offered opposing views on a range of subjects, and it was found that when participants agreed with the perspective they were reading about they spent, on average, 36% more time reading the article.

This selection bias becomes more polarised as people become more committed to their beliefs. An analysis by Valdis Krebs of political book-buying patterns during the 2008 United States presidential election campaign provides a great example.[8] In the five years that he had been analysing these patterns there had always been some books that were purchased by supporters of both parties. However, as polling day approached, the overlap became smaller and smaller until, by October 2008, for the first time in several years of research, Krebs found no overlap – not a single book that appealed to the mindsets of both sides! This mirrored the polarisation and animosity in the campaign rallies of the opponents. People who already supported Obama bought books that had a positive message about him, and vice versa. Since then, we have seen Donald Trump's shock victory in a race that was even more intense and vitriolic. It is hardly surprising, given what we know about confirmation bias, that the 14.2 million Donald Trump supporters who signed up to receive his unfiltered message via Twitter were completely disinterested in attempts by his opponents to discredit him. Such criticism would only appeal to those who already supported Hillary Clinton.

Given this awareness, I hope it is starting to become obvious why "birds of a feather flock together". Think about it: how often do you buy a newspaper or book that you disagree with?

The classic study on how confirmation bias affects our *interpretation* of new information was done in 1979 by researchers from Stanford University.[9] They exposed two groups of volunteers, one that supported capital punishment and one that opposed it, to two different studies (both were fictional, though participants didn't know this), one confirming and one disconfirming their existing beliefs about whether the death penalty deters violent crime.

It would be natural to expect that, if we process information rationally, the additional evidence presented in the articles would lead to a greater understanding of the complexity and trade-offs involved in the decision. It might then seem likely that each group would move closer to the centre-ground. What actually happened was startling. Firstly, when asked to rate the studies, each group had a strong bias towards the one that matched their initial opinion. This led the researchers to conclude that "people of opposing views can each find support for those views in the same body of evidence". Secondly, rather than move together, there was even more polarisation in attitude at the end of the experiment than there had been at the start. It seems that, because of our desire to avoid dissonance, we can read the same information and reach opposite conclusions. Both sides, of course, remain absolutely convinced that they are right.

Other research, such as Leon Festinger's study of Dorothy Martin's little group, shows how powerfully this confirmation bias can lead to the persistence of beliefs even when all supporting evidence has been discredited. Counter-intuitively, information that goes against our point of view can actually make us even more convinced that we are right (and hence the repeated media denouncement of Donald Trump would likely have made his supporters even more certain of their belief in him). As the old saying goes: "a man convinced against his will is of the same opinion still."

So the problem with confirmation bias isn't really what it might look like on the surface: the result of stubborn people consciously ignoring the evidence. If it was, that would be rather easy to deal with for anyone holding an authentic intention to improve their decision making. Rather, the problem is the automatic, unconscious result of how our brains process information. The brain is designed to help us to filter the enormous amount of information that we have to contend with daily, and it does so by paying attention to that which confirms what we already know or believe to be important. And that makes dealing with it a considerable challenge.

In Search of Objectivity

"If you are so sure you are right that you can't even listen to another view ... you're probably wrong."

—Jesse Lyn Stoner

I opened the chapter with a question: how can we know who or what to trust? Can we even trust ourselves? We are faced with a highly ambiguous external environment, with much contradictory information, and, paradoxically, though we live in an age when information has never been so readily available, our desire to cherry-pick what we attend to can make it easier than ever to be misinformed.

I'm sure that you don't need me to remind you that it is a foundation of effective decision making that we need to be sufficiently objective and open-minded to evaluate information impartially. This is relatively easy when we have nothing personally at stake; for example, many people can intelligently weigh evidence and reach a rational conclusion in relation to a dispute between strangers. But when we are involved, it becomes exponentially more difficult to see any other perspective than our own. The more emotionally charged, or the greater the challenge to one of our precious beliefs or values, the more difficult it becomes to be rational and intelligent.

To avoid a challenge to their ideology, some people may get so angry as to shut down its source rather than being willing to consider even the slightest possibility that they are wrong. I could cite so many examples of this that I find it extraordinary that this behaviour doesn't immediately raise warning flags.

We'll look into this in more detail over the next couple of chapters, but here's what it tells us for sure: anyone whose emotions are that far out of control, who has such extreme rigidity and defensiveness around their viewpoint, has already lost their objectivity and as such is highly likely to be wrong. They've proven that they can't face the debate, thereby demonstrating that their opinion must carry enormous bias. Effectively, they have chosen to hang onto their preconceived belief as though it were the mast on a sinking ship, never stopping to consider that their belief might be the hole in the hull (the problems of disease were never going to be solved while hanging on to the idea that bad air was the cause). These people are setting themselves up for disaster.

But just how willing should we be to let go of, or modify, a long-held belief anyway? Naturally, we are likely to err on the side of closed-mindedness, but to reject old beliefs on the first bit of evidence to the contrary feels like an over-compensation. Somehow, we need to find a happy medium – a way of enabling ourselves to give fair consideration to alternative views that takes account of the inherent difficulty of impartially assessing our own opinions.

Part 3 goes into how we can develop the skills we apply to the evidence. But until then, the key question is, *how can we know who or what to trust*? I've presented an argument in this chapter for the power of confirmation bias to justify any existing belief system. Can you even trust that? It may not have escaped your attention that confirmation bias could be at work in the information I've presented here, not only in this chapter but also in the remainder of the book. I can't rule out that possibility, at least not without invalidating my own arguments! Fortunately, in developing the discernment necessary to know what to trust, there are some measures that we can take – fundamental principles of *mindset* – that can go a long way in helping you to improve your judgment and which make me cautiously optimistic that I have been able to overcome the worst effects of confirmation bias in this book:

- The first step in dealing with any type of bias is the awareness of its existence.
- Consciously seek to remain open to opinions that differ from our own. For certain, a negative internal reaction to someone else's opinion needs to be taken very seriously. More on this in Chapter 10.
- Be very cautious in reviewing conflicting information prior to reaching an opinion. Adopt scientific principles for this process; over thousands of years, this is the best approach that mankind has come up with for testing ideas. A hypothesis is a tentative explanation for observed phenomena. The nature of a hypothesis is that it can be refuted, but never proven true, so experiments are designed to rule out hypotheses that are clearly wrong. Each time a hypothesis survives, it gains more credibility, ultimately gaining the status of a theory. Similarly, the more effort you put in to disproving claims about what is true or false, *including your own*, the more confidence you will be able to have in your beliefs. This is critical, and there is a whole section on the subject in Chapter 10.
- Try to be free from conflicts of interest, where you stand to benefit more from one outcome than any other. We've seen how the unconscious mind will tend to move us towards feeling good, even when this is at the cost of truth, so conflicts of interest wreck objectivity.
- Finally, there are some very clear aspects of mindset that predict good judgment and which we can develop deliberately, the most important of which we'll be discussing frequently through the remainder of the book.

So, awareness is the critical starting point upon which everything else gets built, and the next stage in building the awareness necessary for you to improve your decision making is to look at how we process the world around us.

> **Decision-Making Principle #4**
> We have an extraordinary level of ability to convince ourselves that we are right, and to ignore contradictory evidence – even when we are profoundly wrong.

Notes

1. As recorded in their book, *When the Prophecy Fails*, Harper-Torchbooks, 1956. In the book they used the alias Marian Keech to protect Dorothy Martin's privacy.

2. Dr John Ioannidis, Professor of Medicine and of Health Research and Policy at Stanford University School of Medicine, has estimated that as much as 90% of the published medical information that doctors rely on is flawed. His work has been widely accepted by the medical community, having been published in the field's top peer-reviewed journals, and he is one of the most-cited scientists across all scientific literature. His 2005 research paper, "Why most published research findings are false" has been the most downloaded technical paper from the journal *PLOS Medicine*.

3. Editorial Comment, "Offline: What is medicine's 5 sigma?" (2015) *The Lancet*, 385(9976): 1380.

4. Roy Moynihan, "Who pays for the pizza? Redefining the relationships between doctors and drug companies" (2003), *British Medical Journal*, 326(7400): 1189–1192.

5. Jack W. Brehm, "Post-decision changes in desirability of alternatives" (1956) *Journal of Abnormal and Social Psychology*, 52(3): 384–389.

6. Drew Westen, Pavel S. Blagov, Keith Harenski, Clint Kilts and Stephan Hamann, "Neural bases of motivated reasoning: An fMRI study of

emotional constraints on partisan political judgment in the 2004 U.S. presidential election" (2006) *Journal of Cognitive Neuroscience*, 18(11): 1947–1958.

7. Silvia Knobloch-Westerwick and Jingbo Meng, "Looking the Other Way: Selective Exposure to Attitude-Consistent and Counterattitudinal Political Information", *SAGE Publishing*, April 2009.

8. Valdis Krebs, "Your choices reveal who you are: Mining and visualising social patterns", in *Beautiful Visualisation*, O'Reilly Media Inc., 2010.

9. Charles G. Lord, Lee Ross and Mark R. Lepper, "Biased assimilation and attitude polarization: The effects of prior theories on subsequently considered evidence" (1979) *Journal of Personality and Social Psychology*, 37(11): 2098–2109.

5

THE "REALITY" DELUSION

"Everything we hear is an opinion, not a fact. Everything we see is a perspective, not the truth."

—Marcus Aurelius

In the first chapter I introduced the idea that, as human beings, we still retain many "animal instincts", while at the same time generally preferring to think of ourselves as rational. We naturally assume that our conscious experience of the world is "accurate", and that we therefore have a good grasp of what is happening "out there". Since then, I hope you've begun to seriously doubt these beliefs. Now, I'd like to develop a clearer picture of what is going on.

Imagine that you are standing by the side of the road as a police car races towards you with its siren blaring. We all instinctively know that as the car passes the sound made by the siren changes, from a higher pitch as it approaches to a lower one as it moves away. The physics of why this happens is very simple, but even without knowing any physics you still understand what it means. You have perhaps never even given this phenomenon a second thought because it is so familiar and automatic. So, consider this – if there is someone else further down the street who the car hasn't yet reached, the sound they will be hearing won't yet have changed, so they'll literally hear a different "reality" to you. Meanwhile, the police officers sitting in the car will hear yet another pitch, begging the question, what is the actual sound that the siren is making? All three observers are having a different experience, they each have a different version of reality and all are equally correct! The difference is created by what the car is doing *relative to them.*

This scenario highlights three very important aspects of our decision making:

- As we've seen before, instinctive reactions created by unconscious processing can be very useful. In this case, the fact that the pitch changes depending on whether the car is moving towards or away from you will usefully inform a decision about whether the presence of the police car requires some form of action. But what about situations where that isn't the case, where our perception is inaccurate and thereby prompts an inappropriate reaction?
- Perception, and therefore experience, is relative, and since we all have a unique point of observation – relative to the external world and because of the subjective nature of our internal models of the world – the way we see things will always be unique to us.
- We don't actually make decisions based on what is happening *now.* The mind first decides what the current situation implies about what will happen *next* (whether the police car might be a danger to us, needs us to get out of the way, or will never come anywhere near us). It does this by looking for any information from our previous experience that is relevant. If there isn't any, it uses the best approximation that it can, making up a story if necessary. *Our decisions are actually based on an assumption of what will happen next,* and we need to remember how misleading and limiting assumptions can be.

Interpretation Is Subjective

Much has been said and whole books have been written on the idea that the world only affects us through our interpretations or, as Shakespeare put it in *Hamlet*, the demonstrable psychological reality that "[t]here is nothing either good or bad, but thinking makes it so". Conceptually, as long as our ethics and values aren't challenged, this is easy to agree with, isn't it? Ask a room full of people whether they find a roller coaster exhilarating or terrifying (or somewhere in between), and there will be responses from across the spectrum of possibilities. Only the most intolerant of people would not accept that, in this case, no one person's experience is any more "right" or "wrong" than any other's. Here, we are comfortable that our emotional reaction is subjective, the consequence of our own personal interpretation, and that it doesn't need to be challenged or defended.

Unfortunately, this concept – that bad or good depends on perception – gets much harder to accept when it becomes more personal or extreme. What about if you had lost your whole family to the Nazis? I doubt that many people struggle to empathise with the Jews who suffered this experience, but I suspect that even fewer would be able to forgive those responsible. Yet some can and did, even amongst those who had suffered.

Viktor Frankl was a Jewish psychologist who used what he learned from surviving a concentration camp to help others to improve their own lives. His book, *Man's Search for Meaning*, is about the impact that the terrible atrocities the prisoners suffered had on their minds. He noticed that, even in those appalling conditions, there were those who were still able to remain positive and to continue to help others, concluding that these men were proof that:

"Everything can be taken from a man but one thing: the last of human freedoms – to choose one's attitude in any given set of circumstances, to choose one's own way".

That sentence is quite well known as it has been quoted many times. However, for me, the lines that followed are more useful, because they are the ones that point to the "how?":

> *"Every day, every hour, you were offered the opportunity to make a decision, a decision which determined whether you would or would not submit to those powers which threatened to rob you of your very self, your inner freedom".*

Can it be that simple, that the way we feel just comes down to our decisions? I've found that most people initially find this idea very hard to accept, especially when considering extreme circumstances like the one above. It is so natural to blame circumstances or other people when we feel bad, and this idea, that it is we ourselves who shape our inner experience, not the external environment, can be perceived as radical at first. But, it is also transformational. The world had a chance to see this from the way that Nelson Mandela left his 27 years of captivity a completely different man to the one who had entered it. Rightly branded a terrorist when he was imprisoned, he used his captivity to prepare for leadership outside, including making huge shifts in his attitude to his captors. Despite being forced to do hard labour in a quarry, and being confined to a small cell with only a rough bed on the floor and a bucket for a toilet, Robben Island was the crucible for the transformation that enabled him to become widely viewed as one of the greatest leaders of the twentieth century. Let's go deeper.

What Does it All Mean?

Think about this simple question, "Do you beat your partner?"

Well, do you?

I wonder how aware you are of how much your mind has to do so you can respond to that question, starting with establishing its meaning. "Beat" has many potential interpretations, so you had to work out which one I intended. Can you recognise how quickly you did this, almost certainly without even consciously considering the possibilities you rejected because they did not fit with the context, "your partner"? Your interpretation would have been completely different had I asked whether you beat "your eggs" or "your heart". Other possible interpretations, such as those associated with wings or music, were probably seen to be irrelevant even more quickly and effortlessly. But a huge ambiguity still remains ... Did you spot it? Or are you now certain you know what the question was intended to elicit?

I've used this question many times because of how well it illustrates the instinctive way in which *we generate meaning*. In my experience, most people interpret it in one of two ways: either that it is an enquiry about their ability to win in some sort of competitive situation, or alternatively that it relates to whether they ever beat their partner as an act of violence – the second of these being very much the most common. What was your first reaction, and did you realise that there might be an alternative, and very different, way of understanding it?

Clearly, one interpretation – the one to do with winning – would be very benign for most people. For example, for a husband and wife who enjoy playing tennis together, it might create a mild emotional reaction, but this could as easily be positive as negative. However, anyone perceiving the question to be about physical abuse could well feel it to be quite threatening or insulting, especially if they actually had something to hide. Therefore, the subjective experience created by the alternative interpretations could differ widely but, unlike in the case of the police siren, both would *not* be equally "correct" because only one of them would reflect the intention behind the question. The other would lead to a misunderstanding and, very possibly, a completely inappropriate reaction.

Pickpockets and Pockets

So, even the way our mind handles something as simple as the question, "Do you beat your partner?" is far from passive; it cannot be, because the question is ambiguous and we must decide which option to work with. The brain looks for meaning so that it has a basis for deciding what to do next, but what may look like "truth" to us, is really the result of a whole lot of subjective interpretation. You might like to think about this – who would be most likely to infer that the question "do you beat your partner?" had a violent context? Wouldn't it be the person who had done so? And the more guilty about it they felt, or the more afraid of being found out, the more their mind would leap to this conclusion. This is because we naturally interpret everything through the lens of our own experience and belief systems, starting with those experiences that feature most highly in our awareness. I love this old Sufi proverb, because it captures this whole idea so powerfully and in so few words:

"When a pickpocket meets a saint, all he sees are pockets".

Another way of saying this is that *we see the world, not as it is, but as we are.* That might make you uncomfortable, especially if you apply it to the interpretations that you make of others at times, and this is precisely why it is such a potentially transformational understanding. It means that your emotional reaction to any question cannot be attributed to the "reality" of what was asked, any more than a roller coaster can be said to be objectively exhilarating or terrifying. In both cases, *you are actively shaping your reality,* creating the emotion via the *meaning* that you choose to give to what is happening. It means that the way you see others, labelling and judging them, has more to do with you than them, as this wonderful story that I've paraphrased from Stephen R. Covey's book, *The 7 Habits of Highly Effective People*, illustrates:

> Stephen was travelling on the underground when a man got on with his children. The peace and calm that had previously existed was immediately shattered as the children's terrible behaviour disrupted the other passengers. Irritation levels in the carriage understandably started to rise, but the father had closed his eyes and seemed oblivious. Astonished by this obvious lack of sensitivity to others, Stephen spoke politely to the man, suggesting that perhaps he could control his children a little more. The father then seemed to become aware of the situation for the first time, acknowledging he should do something, and saying, "We just came from the hospital where their mother died about an hour ago. I don't know what to think, and I guess they don't know how to handle it either".

If you've not heard this story before, I'm confident that you will have had the experience of seeing things differently. This may be a relatively extreme example but the principle is solid: we experience the meaning we give things, not the situation itself. There is always another interpretation, but as soon as we have gone into judgment, it makes it impossible for us to understand anything at a deeper level. Consider, then, how much greater the potential for misinterpretations and errors must be when faced with the complexity of the modern world.

I hope that these examples demonstrate how much unconscious mental activity is involved in processing even relatively simple situations and giving them meaning, and how much opportunity this introduces for error. This prompts four key questions that identify some huge opportunities to improve our decision making:

1. What determines which interpretation the mind produces first?

2. Knowing how confirmation bias works, how can we get beyond the sense that our first impression is the "right" one?

3. If someone's intention in asking a question did not match our interpretation, cognitive dissonance would tend to lead us to dismiss further explanations that they might be able to add. So, how can we minimise the impact of our own conditioning and develop the capability to seek out and acknowledge alternative perspectives?

4. Given how much of this process happens unconsciously, how can we begin to reduce the subjectivity of our perceptions, to reduce the impact of our personal biases?

The first of these questions will be addressed in the remainder of this chapter, and in the next. The others are central to Part 3. You'll notice that none of these questions is externally focused. Given what we've already covered, including the quotes from Viktor Frankl, I hope this makes sense. As you know from Chapter 1, when things that are hard seem easy, it is because we are using a huge amount of unconscious brain capacity. The more complex and difficult the task in hand, the more we need to rely on the instincts, habits and conditioning wired into unconscious parts of the brain to take care of it – and the capabilities addressed by these questions are definitely complex. Therefore, we should probably expect that the solution will be an internal one. The problem is that once we've conditioned something to the point that it is unconscious, it will tend to determine our results and become very difficult to change.

No Awareness, No Choices

"Until we make the unconscious conscious, it will direct our lives and we will call it fate".

—Carl Jung

Given that we can't hope to improve anything that we are unaware of and, by definition, we must be unaware of activity in the unconscious mind, what can we do?

The answer to this question is simple, even though putting it into practice is definitely not easy: we must raise our level of awareness, gradually becoming more conscious of what is driving the choices that we make. This, above all else that I'm aware of, has the power to transform your decision making. Let's look at a real-world example.

A few years ago I was contacted by someone seeking some coaching support; I'll call her Susan. In our initial consultation, she told me that her main problem was in the area of what is generally called *time management*. She was the managing director of a business that she had taken charge of when it was struggling, had successfully turned around, and then in the subsequent two years had led her team to double its size. The problem was, as the business became larger and more successful, and the number of people reporting to her increased, work was encroaching more and more on her home life. This needed fixing.

We discussed the obvious question early on: did the issue relate to her ability to delegate? Susan demonstrated that she understood the importance of delegation and was unshakable in her belief that she did so effectively. She was also adamant that she wanted a solution, but during the first couple of months nothing was changing. All of my probing to try to understand where the problem lay – why there was such a large difference between what she said wanted and the results she was getting – were coming up against dead ends. The only reality that she could see was that the problem was the result of the enormous workload her job required her to take care of (though she must have believed otherwise at some level, or she wouldn't have hired me!)

I've come across similar problems many times over the years – essentially, people working harder than they say they want to. This belief implies that they have no choice, yet there is always a choice. What is actually driving their behaviour is what they are valuing the most, as that drives decisions about where they spend their time. No one in this situation ever wants to hear it, but if they are spending lots of time at the office while complaining that they don't have more time with the family, it must demonstrate that, in some way, they are getting more out of being at the office than at home. If they weren't, they would choose the family. Nevertheless, understanding the precise reasons for the choice can be very difficult, because the pay-offs from being in the office may not be at all obvious, as was the case with Susan.

Susan and I didn't get to the root cause of her inability to shift her workload until I asked if we could take a look at her diary. I wanted to see if there were any potentially problematic patterns that I could recognise but which she was too close to spot. It seemed to me that she had an unusually large number of meetings with her direct reports. When I asked her what they were for, she said that her team liked to review decisions with her prior to finalising them. Now, this could have been true, but it needed to be challenged. The conversation that followed had a profound impact on many of her decisions moving forwards but, more importantly, it transformed her life:

> Me: "So if that is true [that her team were the driving force behind the number of meetings she had with them] then when you are away, for example when you go on holiday, there would be no problem with you becoming a bottleneck. Is that true? When you are not available, would you be happy for your Directors to make the final decisions despite them not having consulted you?"

There was then a very long pause, one of the longest silences that I've known in my time as a coach. As a leader or coach, if you ask a question of this nature, that stimulates deep thought, it is essential to then stay quiet, because their own answer is the key to maximising learning. Therefore, I let her sit with her thoughts for as long as it took, and these were the next words out of her mouth: "If I do what you are suggesting…". (Don't worry, I'll get to the rest of the sentence in a moment.)

Okay … What had I suggested? Here, we get an insight into the answer to the first of my four questions in the section above (what determines which interpretation the mind produces first?). How had Susan's mind turned my simple question – whether or not it would be okay for her team to press ahead in her absence – into a suggestion? Clearly, her mind had established meaning in the question, but it must have based that meaning on some sort of subjective inference that then shaped her interpretation. What might that have looked like?

Before I offer an answer, let's be clear that we are discussing what *might* have happened in Susan's unconscious here, so the best that I can do is to make inferences myself … I would never dispute that other alternatives are possible. The test of their plausibility is simply whether they adequately explain Susan's perceptions and behaviours.

What seems likely to me, is that Susan quickly realised that the honest answer to my question was "no" (self-honesty is vital to making progress in this type of discussion). This recognition was also conveyed in her body language. Confronted with her own "no", which would have been a bit of a shock since it conflicted with her earlier answers and would therefore have created cognitive dissonance, she probably realised that she wasn't delegating authority to the degree that she had thought. She then perhaps inferred that I had known this all along (I hadn't, although I did think it likely), after which it would only take a small leap of imagination for her to interpret my question as a suggestion. None of this would be a challenge for a mind capable of proving itself right about almost anything.

But that can't have been where Susan left it: that much is obvious from what she said next. She must have gone on to a deeper level of self-inquiry, trying to understand the real reason why she was having all those meetings. Quite possibly she asked herself something like, "If it's not because the team want a second opinion on their decisions, what is driving these meetings?" – the question I'd have asked had she simply said "no" out loud to me! Her answer gave her a huge shift in awareness, identifying an unconscious belief system that had been having a huge impact on her life and profoundly reshaping her interpretation of reality. This was her full statement:

"If I do what you are suggesting, what does the business need me for?"

If you pause for a moment, I expect you will now readily see why it had been so difficult for Susan to let go of the reins sufficiently to achieve her own conscious goals: she'd have had to let go of what she unconsciously felt demonstrated her value to the business. She had genuinely believed that others wanted the meetings, but the truth was that she must have unconsciously communicated to them that she expected major decisions to be reviewed with her before finalisation. We could have talked about time management forever, such as how she could organise her diary more efficiently, but this would have been the equivalent of NASA focusing on fixing the O-rings after the *Challenger* disaster. It wouldn't have affected the key decisions and behaviours that she needed to change, because they were being driven by a much deeper need.

This is why I said above that Susan wanted help with "what is generally called time management". The simple fact is that time management is a misnomer. We cannot manage time: it just trundles on, and we all have the same amount of it. What we must do is to prioritise how to use that time through our decision making, then manage our activities accordingly, a task that may well be affected by much deeper aspects of our psychology than we are conscious of.

The awareness that how we choose to spend our time is determined by what we most need or value in that moment, together with an insight into what was driving her choices, created the possibility for Susan to re-evaluate her decision making and opened up the possibility of finding of a much more powerful solution than was previously possible. She was able to *creatively* identify new ways in which she could add more value than she had been doing while unconsciously micro-managing her direct reports. And here's the beauty of it: once she was able to find such creative solutions, her own behavioural changes were automatic, because the new decisions were still being driven by the same underlying set of values, but now she was able to more fully meet these values. That in turn made work both more fulfilling and enjoyable, and it resulted in her becoming much more effective and successful.

Three Levels of Awareness

So far in this book, I've been referring to mental activity as being simply conscious or unconscious. However, the example in the previous section points to a further distinction that is an essential element in making the changes necessary to transform decision making, because being conscious has two distinct forms. This means that we have three potential states of mind:

Unconsciousness. When you are in this state, your heuristics and conditioning will drive your decision making, because the mind has switched to autopilot. The way you perceive reality will seem like the truth, your emotions will feel "justified", and you'll have no chance of recognising the level of your self-deception or how your emotions are causing imbalance in your brain. In this state, when something happens in the external world, your reaction will be like a reflex – automatic and habitual, able to complete a complex series of programmed actions, but leaving no room for creativity. This is how we can drive home and, having arrived, realise that we have no memory of how we got there. Essentially, when we are unconscious our emotions are in charge, and activity in the higher centres of the brain that are critical to decision making is suppressed.

Awareness. Once you are aware, you can pay attention to the stream of information about the external world that is continuously collected by the senses. This is not a passive process, but rather one that you will need to actively engage in. Now, you will be aware that you are having emotions, although you will most likely believe that they are being "caused" by an external event. Nevertheless, this awareness allows the higher brain to get involved; for example, using judgment to put the emotion in better perspective, memory to assess the results you got from using the emotion in the past, or empathy to consider the impact of the emotion on others. This is the first step in regaining control over the emotions, allowing us to make new and improved choices, but it will only get us so far.

Self-Awareness. The shift from awareness to self-awareness, and the impact that it has on our sense of reality, is huge. With self-awareness we gain the ability to turn our attention inwards, rather than constantly having it pulled towards whatever external event seems most important in the moment. We now have the potential to get to a deeper level of truth, understanding what is driving our emotions and becoming aware of being aware (this is a key concept that I'll return to later). It is also possible for us to profoundly change the way that we see things, giving us the ability to regulate emotions in a new way and to recognise the habitual patterns of thoughts and actions that punctuate all of our lives. With the conscious knowledge of our own character, with all of its beliefs and values, transformation of the inner world that really drives our decisions becomes possible.

In Susan's example above, she was initially completely *unconscious* of the role of her own mind in creating the problem that her life was out of balance. This was demonstrated by the fact that she initially told me that I was not the right coach for her, because she felt that she needed someone who was much more "functional and process orientated" than me! I'm sure you can now judge for yourself the chances of that kind of approach working.

Gradually, as Susan's *awareness* increased, she was able to get to a place where she could recognise and acknowledge that she was not delegating as effectively as she had previously believed – and as you know from the section on confirmation bias in the previous chapter, this acknowledgement is key to making progress. From there, she was able to take the giant leap into the *self-awareness* necessary to recognise what was really driving her choices, the full impact of these choices on herself and others, and why it had been so difficult to change up until that point. Armed with this new level of self-awareness, a whole new realm of possibilities opened up and she became truly empowered to create change in her life.

Notice that when Susan was unconscious, she took her version of reality as a given, accepting that the world "out there" was the source of the problem. But, in fact, the problem was never out there; it was always created "in here". The real limitation was an internal one created by her own mindset.

Given that we can exist in such fundamentally different levels of awareness, it can be no surprise that we can experience so many different variants on, and levels of, truth! We can make rapid progress in our ability to see the world more objectively once we can raise our level of awareness, particularly our self-awareness, of how we are shaping our own perceptions. In fact, these two things – greater objectivity and increased self-awareness – are pretty much inseparable.

Shaping Experience from the Inside Out

"In the space between stimulus (what happens) and how we respond, lies our freedom to choose. Ultimately, this power to choose is what defines us as human beings. It is the choice of acting or being acted upon."

—Stephen R. Covey

The biggest challenge that we must overcome is the one we first looked at in Chapter 1 – the processes involved are totally effortless and almost completely unconscious, making it very difficult to investigate them. Without awareness of how we are creating meaning, what we perceive seems to be a fact beyond question and consequently, for most people, it controls the way they feel. This is the level of *awareness*, and it may sound something like this:

"He made me so mad!"

"She frustrates me to death".

"My work pressures are stressing me out".

"She embarrassed me so badly".

"He totally humiliated me".

"I hate my body".

Notice that all of these statements place the cause outside of one-self – they turn us into a victim and are totally disempowering. So, how can we go from awareness to *self-awareness*, where we have insight (one meaning of which is, literally, to have aware-ness of the inner nature of things) into how we have created the emotion we are experiencing? While a psychologically "accurate" model may not be possible to define, because we are talking about the unconscious, one can be inferred, as I've attempted to do in Figure 5.1.

My hope is that with this model, we can now piece together sev-eral discussions that we've looked at in other parts of the book, to reach an inescapable conclusion that *perception isn't passive.* Contrary to our conditioning, which leads us to believe that we are directly aware of the outside world, as though our eyes oper-ate just like a camera, there are actually multiple ways in which we actively shape what we see and hear:

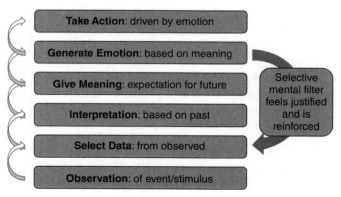

Figure 5.1

- The starting point in the process is that something "out there" is perceived through the senses and filtered by a set of internal rules or beliefs. We saw in the previous chapter how powerful these filters can be, in extreme cases even allowing people to ignore information that would enable them to see a doomsday prediction for what it is. Because of these filters, we will always tend to see what we already believe – our confirmation bias. Thus the young boy bitten by a dog, who now has a belief that dogs are dangerous, has his attention drawn to every dog that he comes across.
- Having selected what to place attention on, we refer to the past to interpret the significance of the event – for the young boy, "this animal is dangerous".
- The interpretation then allows us to evaluate what the situation means for us in the future – "I could get hurt (again)".
- The emotion is a natural consequence of the meaning we generated – e.g. "I'm afraid". Once this emotion has got a hold on us, it then reinforces what we see, deepening the self-deception of our objectivity (we'll look at the impact of fear in much greater depth in Chapter 6), and making it difficult to recognise alternative perspectives. Effectively, our own mental processing determines our emotional experience, which then justifies that the original interpretation was correct!
- As we saw in the section on *motivated reasoning* in the last chapter, and in the example of how Susan's unconscious beliefs affected some very big decisions, the emotion will have a major effect on how we behave.

Nothing escapes this process of reality making, but the more attention we are able to give to the three stages between the observation and the experience of emotion, the more we will come to understand, for example, that it is impossible for anyone else to "make me mad". This idea would then naturally become replaced with something like, "I am feeling angry". While we often cannot choose what happens to us, as Viktor Frankl pointed out, we can always decide to change our experience of it because:

> *"Reality"* is not something that we perceive; it is something that we *create in our mind.*

Making choices at this level is decision making at its most profound. Now your reality can shift, enabling you to regain control over your inner world and become truly empowered to make changes. What's more, the deeper you take your self-awareness (and I'll be explaining how to do this in Part 3), the more power you will have to change your perceptions. In the next chapter we'll explore the practical aspects of why all of this matters so much.

Decision-Making Principle #5
It is impossible to experience "reality", or to be "objective", because everything is processed unconsciously prior to awareness. By shifting our perception of "reality", we will automatically start to make new choices.

6

WIRED FOR FLIGHT AND FIGHT

"The enemy is fear. We think it is hate; but it is really fear."
—Mahatma Gandhi

If we are not the receivers of a fixed reality, but rather the shapers of it, what should we seek to shape in order to help us to improve our decision making? How do we need to learn to see the world and, given that perception is an inside-out process, what does our inner model need to look like to achieve this?

In Chapter 2, I sought to reinforce the essential nature of the need for proactive change. Quite possibly, you had a good awareness of this already; it is hard to read much these days without getting messages about volatility and disruption. Indeed, many excellent books have been written on this subject, such as *Team of Teams*, by the leader of the war against Al Qaida in Iraq, General Stanley McChrystal, and *Only the Paranoid Survive*, by former Intel CEO, Andy Grove. So, the issue in handling change effectively is not *awareness* of the need, but rather most people's lack of *self-awareness* of:

- the reason why our access to the capabilities necessary to handle effectively the pressures of change has a tendency to decrease in proportion to the need for them; in other words, just when we most need our greatest adaptability, resilience and creativity is when they are least available to us

• where to start in seeking to create the internal changes of mindset that are needed.

It's a classic case of the knowing–doing gap in action, stemming from the same root cause as the relative rarity of "common sense". Clearly, it is not much help to know something if the new decisions arising from that awareness don't create beneficial new behaviours. To close the gap we need to take a closer look inside the brain, particularly at the interaction between the older, instinctive and emotional parts of the brain and the new kid on the block, the intellectual, thinking part that "knows". We need to better understand this relationship and learn how to optimise brain activity for higher performance. Let's start with the older bits.

Is Survival About Paranoia?

In Andy Grove's book, *Only the Paranoid Survive* (a phrase that also became his management dictum), the primary message seems to be a warning against complacency, particularly in the face of ongoing major changes that Grove calls strategic inflection points, and a reminder of the importance of innovation (hopefully, this is not my own confirmation bias!). There can't be much doubt that this is extremely sound advice. It's the same message as the one from Lou Gerstner that we looked at in Chapter 2, which he referred to using the term *the success syndrome.*

Paranoia is "a tendency on the part of an individual or group toward excessive or irrational suspiciousness and distrustfulness of others". People suffering from it basically believe, without evidence or justification, that others are out to get them or trying to harm them. It derives from the Greek word for madness. It is implicit that it involves thoughts driven by anxiety and fear, often to the point of delusion or irrationality, where the person affected perceives threats all over the place.

This hardly seems like a healthy mind state for good decision making, yet Andy Grove was clearly a very good decision maker, being instrumental in building Intel into the world's largest manufacturer of semiconductors, *Time* magazine's "Man of the Year" in 1997, and one of the greatest influences on the worldwide electronics manufacturing industry. He said: "The things I tend to be paranoid about vary. I worry about products getting screwed up, and I worry about products getting introduced prematurely. I worry about factories not performing well …"[1] This list of things he worries about goes on for quite a while … But "worry", while still negative, is not the same as paranoia, not remotely the same. Paranoia is worry or anxiety on steroids.

So, what about paranoia? Is it the solution to survival? Does it have a useful role to play in our decision making? And what about less intense fear-based emotions, like worry and anxiety? What impact do they have on our decisions and what type of actions do they create? These are important questions, because there is a lot of fear in the world today, and I showed in the previous chapter how the emotions we are experiencing affect the way we filter the world, and thereby our overall perceptions, in a closed loop process which then reinforces the original emotion creating more and more of the same. Because of this, if we are on the wrong track, time will likely make our results worse rather than better.

Our Evolutionary Heritage

Although a lot of stress these days is dysfunctional, at its root, stress makes perfect sense: it is our instinctive biological response to fear. The reaction itself is probably prehistoric, because we can see that it is triggered in a primitive area of the brain which is an inheritance from our pre-human past. Even the most ancient organisms display this type of response, despite lacking the complex brains that many species have today, and we can see it in all animals.

For animals in the wild, survival depends on remaining constantly alert to their surroundings for any sign of a threat, and a specialised part of the brain, called the amygdala, developed to handle this capability. If a gazelle gets the slightest hint of a tiger in the vicinity, its amygdala triggers a response, via another part of the brain called the hypothalamus which looks after some of our most basic drives; this then activates all of the bodily systems necessary to mobilise as much energy as possible to enable it to flee. This is a perfect "adaptive" response in those circumstances. In other species, this same energy would enable them to prepare to, quite literally, fight for their lives. Hence its name: the fight-or-flight mechanism. We also call it the threat response or stress response.

When this reaction gets triggered, its effect throughout our body is remarkable. Muscles get prepared for action as extra blood is pumped to them. Heart rate and breathing are optimised for maximum physical performance. The senses become heightened and the mind is tuned to be super-alert. Concentration intensifies. Non-essential bodily processes, like digestion and repair, cease (it is not the time to digest a meal when you are about to be eaten!), and feelings of hunger and thirst subside. And in human beings, one other thing also happens that has a critical impact on decision making: *we stop thinking.*

With the activation of the threat response, brain activity changes as blood is channelled into the hind brain and away from the forebrain. This hind brain deals with automatic reactions, so that we can maximise our ability to cope with what is happening right now, whilst the forebrain is like the captain of the ship, giving us the potential to set a new course: to *think, then react.*

If the Only Tool You Have is a Hammer ...

Psychologist Abraham Maslow is quoted as saying: "I suppose it is tempting, if the only tool you have is a hammer, to treat everything as if it were a nail." This is a great metaphor for the idea that anyone armed only with a narrow worldview will tend to want to see problems, and their solutions, through that restricted focus. If a child is given a toy hammer as a gift, his one strategy is likely to be to bash anything that comes within arm's reach, which may be great fun but will rarely be appropriate. Higher awareness makes it obvious that different tools are needed for different jobs.

Unfortunately, the part of the brain that triggers the fight-or-flight mechanism is a bit like the child with the hammer – the only variable it has is how hard to hit its target. When we are not at risk of being eaten, we still behave as though we are, which creates a "maladaptive" response: the effect of fear promoting inappropriate actions and behaviours. Phobias provide great examples for us to look at, because the move into survival mode is so strong and easy to see, and because they highlight just how dysfunctional our minds become once they are in a fearful state.

Fearing "Nothing"

"Fear is only as deep as the mind allows."

—Japanese proverb

A phobia is an excessive and irrational fear reaction to a thing or situation. In terms of the level of their irrationality, phobias are very similar to paranoia, except that in the case of paranoia the fear is created by nothing more than a concept or belief, whereas with a phobia people have something tangible that they can blame for the feeling!

Extreme, overwhelming and debilitating fear can be triggered by a phobia. For example, I've had people in workshops who lose the ability to function simply because I put a picture of a spider on the screen. Sometimes, their mind becomes so overcome with fear that they cannot even talk about whether they are behaving rationally, nor respond to basic questions, until the picture is removed. Essentially, they have become completely *unconscious*. It is, literally, as though they are faced with a tiger from which they cannot escape. Figures differ between sources, but as many as 10% of people may suffer from a phobia at any one time, with up to 20% experiencing a specific phobia at some point in their life.

A great example of the debilitating nature of excessive fear created by a phobia came up in one of my workshops recently. When I asked if anyone had a phobia, one man, I'll call him Pete, said that he was terrified of butterflies and moths (he's not alone: a fear of moths is called mottephobia). As an example, he cited a recent meal out with friends when, 20 minutes or so into the meal, he noticed a moth on the wall close to where they were sitting. The conversation from that point went something like this:

Me: "I'm guessing the meal didn't taste too good after that?"

Pete: "I couldn't eat at all after that." (By this time he had a distinct red flush spreading up his neck.)

Me: "And yet, there was nothing wrong for the first 20 minutes?"

Pete: "No."

Me: "So the issue was nothing to do with the moth then?"

At this point Pete hesitated, looking confused, before he said, "Of course it was the moth."

Me: "The moth was there all the time – that hadn't changed. So how could it have been the moth?"

Pete: (After a long pause) "That feels rather uncomfortable."

Me: "Great. That's a good sign you have the opportunity to learn something. Where is the true source of the problem then?"

Pete: (Reluctantly) "It must be in my mind."

I love working with people like Pete (and Susan, from the previous chapter), who are willing to be honest, open and somewhat vulnerable, because these are key requirements for achieving progress. It is clear that his particular version of reality was very different to the majority of other people's and that, more importantly, it did not serve him in any useful way.

As we moved on, I was hoping that he wouldn't notice the butterflies that I use in my logo, which were watermarked onto the pages of the handout that I'd given him. It wasn't to be. A few minutes later he put the handout down, face down on the table, with a look of discomfort, but now with a hint of bemusement at the recognition of what his own mind was doing to him. Phobias like this demonstrate that even when there is literally nothing to fear, our minds are quite capable of being afraid of "nothing".

The Scary Unknown

"With all the rhetoric about how management is about change, the fact is that we managers loathe change, especially when it involves us."

—Andrew S. Grove

Not only do we have the ability to create fear out of nothing, our brain is also wired to do so when we are unsure. It will activate our fight-or-flight mechanism to protect us from the discomfort of the unknown.

Back to the gazelle. When its grazing is interrupted by a rustle from the undergrowth, its fight-or-flight mechanism is immediately triggered, and all of its attention gets pulled onto the external environment so that it can determine whether or not there is a potential threat. Its brain searches for patterns it recognises, and when there is one – like a tiger – it knows exactly what to do.

Clearly, evolution couldn't prepare the gazelle for everything it might encounter, so what happens if it sees something new and unknown, such as a poacher with a gun? Survival can't take chances, so any experience that cannot be mapped to something with which the animal is already familiar and is known to be safe, will be treated as a potential threat until proven to be otherwise. It has to be this way, because the price of incorrectly assuming something to be safe might be death. Thus, even the outline of a rock that looks as though it could be a tiger has to be treated as a tiger. It takes time, and repeated non-threatening exposure, for the animal to learn, through conditioning, that fight-or-flight is not required. This is why the gorilla researcher must spend weeks or months quietly observing a troop from a distance, building trust before edging closer. Approaching too quickly could easily lead to death.

Given our neurological inheritance and the fact that very deep wiring handles the stress response, it is no surprise that, here too, our core nature is like other animals: *we also naturally experience the unknown as a threat.* This is why most people would have a very different experience walking along the same path through the woods during the day to how it would be at night, or why going downstairs at night is very different to normal if you are worried about the source of a strange noise that has just woken you up. Fear results in something that we were merely uncertain about being swapped for the worst case scenario.

Decades of research, including social psychology experiments, election polls and cross-cultural comparisons, indicate that this fear of the unknown also has a profound impact on our relationships. This work has enabled psychologists to deduce that when we meet someone for the first time, the first priority in our mind is to determine whether they are friend or foe. We want to know what their intentions are towards us, because we are seeking to establish whether we are safe with them. What's more, because it relates to survival, it turns out that we are very good at it! When people are asked to judge faces which they have seen for less than 4/100ths of a second, they assess those traits that help us to determine intention (such as morality, trustworthiness, sincerity, kindness and friendliness) more reliably than any others.[2]

We can do the incredibly complex task of assessing a face effortlessly, in a fraction of a second, by leveraging the power of the instinctive capabilities we looked at in Chapter 1. Similarly, think what would happen if you were in the jungle and heard a rustle in the undergrowth. Just like the gazelle, your brain would instantly assume it to be a threat and seek to work out where the sound came from, doing so much faster than the time it takes to think about it.

Just as our brain is primed to process the unknown rustle in the undergrowth as danger, our starting point when meeting a newcomer is the same: to assume them to be a threat until proven otherwise. To our animal brain, it is purely a matter of self-preservation. So it is natural for us to react unconsciously to the unknown, in a split-second, before the rational mind has even had time to become engaged.

Warped Perceptions

Because stress and the hormones that it triggers don't change their basic operation as the emotional dial gets turned up, we know that lower level fears have the potential to stimulate essentially the same reactions, even if their lack of intensity makes it much less obvious. This is particularly true if lots of small stresses build up to a critical point, after which even the smallest setback, in our jobs, relationships, financial situation, health, and even our imagination, can easily trigger a full-blown fight-or-flight response. We have a seemingly unlimited capability to create a "tiger" out of practically anything:

- Someone takes your parking space or bumps into you with their shopping trolley.
- A text message from the boss asking you to come to her office.
- People who look different.
- Sitting in rush hour traffic or a delayed train!
- A look of disapproval (especially from someone like your spouse).
- Call centres.
- A meal in a restaurant that you don't approve of.

You get the picture ... all of these things have a fear hiding in the background and, like the child with the toy hammer, this gives them the potential power to squeeze out everything else. Once something has triggered us, we effectively become like an amped-up animal, only able to concentrate on the three things that are of the greatest importance for survival:

1. To ensure our physical safety, the body must take priority – it needs to be protected. This is why, frequently, when people's stress levels are not appropriate for the external stress that they are facing, they have a tendency to

become overly obsessive about their weight or how they look. The attention that is being directed towards the body must be focused on something! It also explains why stress causes people to become so selfish – there is no room in our minds for others when we are struggling to survive.

2. Like a hyper-vigilant wild animal that has sensed danger, we become highly fixated on the environment, the goal being to detect and then evade the threat. This explains why people who are stressed are always looking for a cause outside themselves. They constantly see problems, rather than creatively looking for solutions, because a future solution is of no relevance to a survival issue taking place right now. They also struggle to listen effectively to others – their mind is literally elsewhere and someone else's problems will be very far down their priority list.

3. It makes perfect sense that when faced with a real threat we would need to rapidly establish how long we have to escape. Consequently, stress produces an obsession with time, most likely creating the feeling that there will never be enough of it and making it very difficult to even consider taking the time to relax. So, unfortunately, when we are stressed, we block ourselves from the thing that we need most – allowing ourselves time for recovery.

Driven by these priorities we become control freaks, attempting to shape everything in our life to be as we want it, in order to restore balance, harmony and comfort.

Given this extreme narrowing of focus, it is hardly surprising that nothing has the power to distort our perception of reality more than fear. Once our mind gets working this way, it is inevitable that we will become excessively self-interested, miss many important decision-making cues that are available to us, become devoid of the ability to seek new perspectives and lose our objectivity.

There are few, if any, solutions to the complex problems of the modern world that arise from a survival orientation. Most daily decisions today require the thinking, rational brain, not its emotional cousin whose aggressive over-reactivity and hyper-vigilance will tend to cause behaviours that are counter-productive to survival. It is no surprise that it is difficult to make decisions effectively once fear or anxiety kicks in, or that the paranoid struggle to function in the world in any sort of normal way!

Imagine if we could learn to channel that same capability more positively. Thankfully we can, and the knowledge we are currently building will help you to do so. In Part 3, we'll look in detail at how to put it all into practice.

Creating Stress by Thought Alone

"If you are distressed by anything external, the pain is not due to the thing itself, but to your estimate of it; and this you have the power to revoke at any moment."

—Marcus Aurelius

We all experience brief periods of stress, but much evidence indicates that more and more people are suffering stress in a way that interferes with their ability to function normally over an extended period. Perhaps this is not surprising, given that uncertainty in the modern world is on the increase, and how easily we can create the perception of a threat.

The fears created this way have nothing to do with our thinking brains, which have been pushed into the background. Because they make no rational sense, in situations where survival is not at stake they play havoc with our decision making. Pretty soon, just as we can condition ourselves to be afraid of a specific event or object, we can develop a generalised sense of fear or anxiety, or perhaps even paranoia. When this happens, fear becomes the lens through which we see the world.

Clearly, this mindset is highly maladaptive. The greater the stress, the larger the gap will be between how things are and how they appear to us, and the more inappropriate will be our reaction. Decisions taken during such times will rarely be good ones and may be catastrophic, as anyone who has ever fired back a rapid reply to an email that has annoyed them will no doubt confirm. Therefore, the more effectively we can learn to handle such fears, the better our decisions will become. Yet, this pattern does demonstrate the incredible power of our brain, which is easily able to create fear from nothing, and potentially intensify it until it becomes a phobia, through thought alone.

So, let's get to a deeper level of truth in relation to paranoia and phobias. Although I started out by making a distinction between them, saying that in the case of phobias there is something to blame, while paranoia is more conceptual, now we can see that they actually have the same root cause: dysfunctional use of the creativity of the mind. This means that, potentially, they also have the same solution, and so do the more routine levels of fear that we can all experience. The key is to realise that anything that we place our attention on expands in our awareness, even if that thing is nothing more than a figment of our imagination. That is how we created them in the first place. And if we created the fear, why shouldn't it be possible for us to undo it again by the same method?

This suggests that if we can learn to control attention, we can change how we perceive things. Then, as we covered in the last chapter, what we call reality must change too. This is true transformation:

Now, we are no longer limited to a single option for handling stressors which, as the famous book title by Susan Jeffers suggested, is to "feel the fear and do it anyway". Now, we can learn to modulate the fear at root cause, reducing or removing it completely.

I realise that is a big statement, so I had better justify it. The most basic response of the brain is the startle reflex. It is triggered in the hypothalamus (the same part that precipitates the stress response), which sits in the brain stem, the very oldest part of the brain. Its sole purpose is protection. We don't have to think to blink or dodge our head sideways if a fly approaches our eye, or to move our hand from a hot stove. This very basic reaction takes just 20 milliseconds, and used to be considered to be beyond voluntary control or intentional modification.

Meditation is essentially a practice of focusing attention in a specific way. Studies with highly experienced meditators have shown that they have developed the capability to modulate even the most primitive brain activity. In one study,[3] the researchers had to extend the scale for measuring the intensity of the facial reactions they were monitoring, because the startle response of the participant was so low. The conclusion of the authors was that "engaging in meditation can modulate a reflexive response that is located in quite primitive regions of the human nervous system".

The Problem in a Nutshell

It's not too hard to spot the problem we've been working through in this chapter is it? Let me sum it up, because it provides the basis for what we must do in Part 3.

How many challenges do you face in the world today of the "flee or get eaten" variety? But the amygdala processes everything in terms of survival, so when it perceives a threat it tries to take over – and it has the ability to do so before we've even had a chance to think. This isn't conscious, it's biological. To make matters worse, we don't even need a genuine threat in order to become stressed. Like Pavlov's dogs, or the wife who was cutting the ends off the ham without understanding why, conditioning is automatic, and it can activate our fight-or-flight mechanism in response to practically anything once something has caused us to get wired that way. We need to find a way around the fact that:

- On the one hand, most modern world problems require us to think. They are unpredictable and ambiguous, constantly presenting new tests that require a creativity-based approach to dealing with them. Overall, they are much more complex than our fight-or-flight mechanism can handle.
- On the other hand, to the degree we become stressed by these problems, our brain wants to try to handle them just as it would a tiger. Uncertainty itself creates fear, so it is pretty much inevitable that just when we most need our creative capabilities, the brain will block access to precisely these mental resources.

This dilemma is clearly evident from the example of Pete's phobia of moths that we looked at earlier. His intellect is easily sufficient for him to run a business, but this is not about his intelligence. Furthermore, he already knew, before his conversation with me, that his fear was absurd and irrational – in other words he had reached the level of *awareness*. However, the presence of a moth would continue to seem to him as though it was the "cause" of his feelings, leaving him as a victim of his circumstances, with no ability to create change. But, with the deeper level of truth arising from the *self-awareness* of the real source of the problem – the mind – the possibility of finding a solution opened up.

We can see that, with Pete's new level of awareness, the nature of the challenge of improving his decision making changes: from dealing with the moth, to loosening the grip of his emotional brain. *It is a shift from an external to an internal focus.* Once his emotional brain had taken over, it didn't care what the intellect had to say on the subject – we could say that he wasn't having the emotion, but rather, that the emotion had him, because he was gripped by it, completely unable to control it.

I like to describe this challenge as moving from *reaction* to *response*. It is important to recognise that the standard terms we've been using – the threat response, or stress response – are actually reactions rather than responses, because they are unconscious and deeply conditioned as opposed to being true responses which involve an element of conscious choice. I've been referring to them as responses only to remain consistent with the normal terminology, and I will continue to do so. But this is a critical distinction, because it is the ability to make conscious choices, as highlighted in the section about Viktor Frankl in Chapter 5, which gives us the potential to overcome our habits and conditioning.

I hope that the two stages required to improve your decision making are now clear:

- First, self-awareness is required, which is what much of the first two parts of this book have been about. We will continue this journey in Part 3.
- Second, we need to learn how to gain greater control over how our brain is operating, so that we can maximise our ability to act adaptively. But because of the power of our instincts, particularly when the unconscious perceives a threat, this isn't just a matter of deciding to. We cannot simply will ourselves to see things more positively, and therefore a deeper level solution is required.

Decision-Making Principle #6
Stress drives maladaptive choices and decisions, so the reduction of stress will tend to improve decision making.

Notes

1. Andrew S. Grove, *Only the Paranoid Survive*, HarperCollins Publishers, 1996, p. 3.
2. Moshe Bar, Maital Neta and Heather Linz, *Very First Impressions*, American Psychological Association, 2006.
3. Robert W. Levenson, Paul Ekman and Matthieu Ricard, *Meditation and the Startle Response: A Case Study*, PMC, 2013.

7

THE DANCE OF OLD AND NEW

"The only really valuable thing is intuition."

—Albert Einstein

Few would disagree with the idea that Albert Einstein was one of the most influential physicists of the modern age, a great visionary whose intuitive leaps often took years to prove mathematically. Such was Einstein's farsightedness that his reputation and stature in the world of physics grew even more in the decades following his death, as physicists gathered more evidence to support his theories. He was also known as a philosopher and humanist, and the breadth of his insights is readily evident from the many quotations by him that still circulate in popular culture.

Equally, Thomas Edison is pretty much unanimously viewed as one of the greatest inventors of modern times, perhaps of all time. His products, including the phonograph, the incandescent light bulb, the telegraph, alkaline batteries, and one of the earliest motion picture cameras, transformed the world.

These two men had in common an astonishing proficiency in using a critical mental quality that we've talked about in a general way already – *creativity*. This is a very different capability to the intellect, and one that is not accessible by trying, or will power.

How do Einstein, Edison and people like them – Archimedes, da Vinci, Michelangelo, Mozart, Tesla and more – get to be so creative? Does it come down to a natural "talent", or can we all learn to be more like them? And if we can learn, what does it take to do so?

Scientific research gives a quick answer on the first point: we *can* learn how to improve our creativity. The starting point to answer the second question is where we left off in the previous chapter: to improve our decision making we need to gain greater control over the mind, to increase our ability to respond rather than react, because reactivity and creativity are at opposite ends of the same spectrum. To understand how to do this, we'll need a model of how the mind works.

Modelling the Mind

There are many potential models we could use. A very common one builds on the fact that the natural priority of our brains is to keep us alive, which means deciding whether the world around us represents a threat or an opportunity. We know that even subtle levels of perceived danger can have a significant impact on how we think, driving us into reactive states, unless we can learn to manage our emotions better. In this dual-process model, based on the combination of the old, reactive emotional system and our newer, rational mind, these two systems are usually seen as being at odds with each other, battling for supremacy. While this approach can be very helpful for looking at reactivity, it doesn't provide the base we need to become more creative and, as you'll see, these two systems are highly complementary when used properly.

Another common way of looking at the mind, sometimes called the "blink" versus "think" model, draws its primary distinctions from the relative thinking speeds that can be observed. In Daniel Kahneman's classic book, *Thinking Fast and Slow*, he used the terms System 1 and System 2 to describe the two systems in the mind, with System 1 being the fast, automatic, effortless unconscious and System 2 being the slow, familiar, rational, effortful conscious. Again, we have a dual-system model, but this time it naturally includes intuitive feelings and enables a great understanding of how rationality and snap judgments interact. It also explains why the intuition can fail so spectacularly at times. However, it doesn't distinguish very clearly between the different forms of fast thinking that we've discussed in this book:

- *Instincts and heuristics*, including our fight-or-flight mechanism, which are passed on as part of our genetic inheritance.
- *Learned skills*, where we have become conditioned to act reflexively to external events in a particular way. This conditioning could be consciously chosen and developed, such as the way that Andy Murray hits a tennis serve or Nicola Benedetti plays her violin, or learned unconsciously, like almost all phobias.
- *Creative leaps*, such as those achieved by Frederick Winslow Taylor, David Cook, Reed Hastings, Tobaru Kobayashi or Dick Fosbury.

Another popular approach to modelling the mind is to base it on a highly simplified view of the anatomy of the brain, which enables us to take the best of both models outlined above. While we need to be clear that the mind and the brain are different – you'll see later that the mind can change the brain, so they must be – a simple understanding of what is going on in the brain offers insights that can help enormously in understanding what we can do to better use our mind.

The Three Part Brain

The model we are going to start with is commonly known as the Triune Brain (Figure 7.1), based on the work in the 1960s of Dr Paul MacLean. From both neuroanatomical and evolutionary perspectives, more recent research has highlighted significant technical errors with this model, so please don't use this model as the basis for an argument with a neuroscientist, because you'll lose. Nonetheless, it is useful as one of very few simple approximations of the truth on offer.

The essence of the model is that each of the three parts represents a different phase of our evolution, performing distinctive functions and driven by different priorities.[1] As we step through the parts, I'll seek to link each one to the functions of mind that we've discussed thus far, so that we can build an integrated picture of the whole.

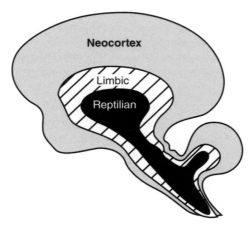

Figure 7.1

1. THE INSTINCTIVE STAGE

Our evolution began with the instinctive part of the brain, in this model referred to as the "reptilian" brain, or brain stem. Refined over more than 500 million years, the instinctive capabilities that are evident in much of what we do are based here. They cannot be explained through mental rules that we are aware of at a conscious level and have the simple goal of ensuring our survival. The *heuristics* that we looked at in Chapter 1 are an important part of this capability. Also housed here are the fight-or-flight mechanism that we discussed in the last chapter and bodily functions that occur naturally, such as hunger, thirst and the desire to reproduce (easy to remember as the four Fs – fight, flight, feed and fornicate).

Also in here, in a part called the cerebellum, is control of learned, coordinated and memorised actions, like hitting a tennis ball, playing the violin or recognising aircraft far away in the distance. Little or no conscious memory is required to perform these actions once they have been practised enough to master them.

Whether pre-programmed or learned, because these functions are subconscious, we are pretty much blind to the mental activity that controls them and, if we let them, they will attempt to drive our life on automatic pilot. This part of the brain generates impulses to act, based on attraction and avoidance, but has no ability to judge them.

2. THE EMOTIONAL STAGE

Next in our evolution came the development of the emotional brain, or limbic system (which is actually made up of a set of diverse structures), somewhere between 300 and 150 million years ago. It is also referred to as the "mammalian" brain. It is the base of our emotions, as well as being important to short-term memory and smell. It gives us the ability to experience feelings associated with the four Fs, and also has an important function in storing information to long-term memory, which is why we remember things better when they are associated with strong emotions.

Throughout Part 2, I have been seeking to demonstrate the impact that emotions can have on our decision making. While the instinctive brain produces the basic "towards" and "away" motivations associated with desire and fear, these can be mediated in the limbic system so that we experience a rich variety of emotions, from love to hate and envy to celebration. Importantly, because we can name these emotions, and have a natural desire to understand them, they start to move us away from an existence based purely on survival and begin our shift into awareness. However, the focus of this part of the brain is our internal state which, as we saw in the last couple of chapters, may well be extremely maladaptive. To then amplify the problem, this focus subsequently makes the emotion self-sustaining. Again, at this level, we have no ability to recognise when our own mental processes are not serving us.

Both the instinctive and emotional brains are *reactive*, demanding action. Being subconscious, they are heavily affected by habits and biases, leading to the repetition of old thoughts and behaviours – there is no potential for anything new here! That is what reactivity means: we re-act to something that is either picked up through the senses or envisaged purely in the mind, relying on a set of rules that is already deeply programmed into our brain.

3. THE INTELLECTUAL STAGE

The newest part of the brain is the so-called neocortex (the prefix *neo* meaning new or modified). In relative terms, its growth is very recent, beginning only about 3 million years ago, yet it makes up about 90% of the overall cortex. With it came the development of the intellect and a major advance in capability – rationality. The neocortex enables us to take a step back from both external events and our inner state and to analyse them consciously, with focus and concentration, and thereby to break free of old reactive patterns. It also gives us the ability to learn, memorise and reason. As a result, we have the capacity for what is normally called "free will"; in other words, because of our intellect, we can make *conscious decisions*.

Let's have a quick look at how this works. Why would you listen to music or go to the cinema? Obviously, such things must be enjoyable because of the emotions that they stimulate, or you wouldn't bother. We enjoy our emotions (the ones we want, at least), and when we go to the cinema we can experience a wide range of them without risk. I wonder, when was the last time you were enjoying some music, or a movie, and reflected on why you were enjoying it? Rarely, if ever? The whole point is that we get caught up in our emotional experiences. But if you were absorbed in some music and I were to ask what you were doing, by the time you answered you would no longer be absorbed – now, you would be thinking! The question prompts a shift in focus, and the thinking it stimulates creates the possibility of a new decision. That thinking takes place in the neocortex.

So, while the intellectual mind can be seen to be the seat of our conscious awareness, it is also very easy to take for granted, because thinking is so intrinsic to who we are as human beings and because it, too, can become habitual and unconscious. It has been estimated that we probably have upwards of 50,000 or 60,000 thoughts per day, and that, for most of us, more than 90% of them will be the same ones that we had yesterday. This is not really thinking – it is just reactive mental activity. Fortunately, we can break out of it by thinking about our thinking.

There's a name that is commonly given to thinking about thinking: *metacognition*. It incorporates all of the processes used to plan, monitor and assess our understanding and performance. This is the route to the new conscious choices discussed in Chapter 6. Researchers have found[2] that when metacognition is weak, "people tend to be blissfully unaware of their incompetence", lacking "insight about deficiencies in their intellectual and social skills". Conversely, used properly, thinking is the only way to create a dramatic increase in awareness, specifically, the development of self-awareness through the deliberate focusing of attention. This is what I call *intentional attention*, and I believe the development of it to be the ultimate skill, because not only does it provide the basis for advancing every other skill, it is also the mechanism by which we can change our mind, as we'll see in Chapter 10.

Overall then, the intellect, and the rational thought that it enables, has had a transformational effect on our decision making, freeing us from being totally gripped by our instincts and emotions. However, there is still a major gap because, while this capability can explain how, for example, the efficiency of the Industrial Revolution was honed over time, it offers no explanation of the source of Einstein or Edison's creativity, or of where Frederick Winslow Taylor's idea for his revolution came from in the first place. Something more is clearly necessary.

Two Approaches to Decision Making

"I began to realise that an intuitive understanding and consciousness was more significant than abstract thinking and intellectual logical analysis. Intuition is a very powerful thing, more powerful than intellect, in my opinion."

—Steve Jobs

In Part 1 of this book I laid out the transformation that is taking place from the predictability of the industrial age model of business to the volatile and ambiguous environment of today. I described *simple*, *complicated* and *complex* systems in Chapter 3, highlighting that *complex* environments are becoming much more prevalent.

Many of the problems that arise in *simple* and *complicated* situations can of course be solved using the memory: their repeatability means that most problems will have been seen before in a very similar form. This approach, based on previous experience, is probably the best known and understood method of making decisions, which we could call "*problem solving*". This is the essence of our education system: remember and repeat. To learn mathematics, students are taught a range of problem-solving approaches, which they memorise, after which their job is to work out which solution to apply to each problem. No one is expected to arrive at probability theories, calculus, differential equations, or even basic algebra, on their own.

Applied to the business environment, at the more basic end of the simple–complicated spectrum, not much is at stake, there will be few possibilities, and there will be a clear cause–effect relationship; little intelligence is required to apply a problem-solving approach to any challenges that arise here. However, at the other end of the spectrum, high levels of expertise are essential, because there will be many variables and potential outcomes, and that introduces the need for trade-offs. There are no shortcuts to accumulating the broad spectrum of knowledge necessary to address complicated problems; it takes time, wide-ranging experience and the ability to embed the learning from that experience into memory.

The use of memory to address problems, however, introduces a potential problem. Once a rat has learnt how to run through a maze to find its food, it simply accesses its memory bank of previous experience to do it again. But if the maze changes or someone moves the food, the rat will initially be caught out by its unquestioned assumption that its old strategy will work. This is the real danger of habits: they enable only reactivity, offering no ability to cope with change. Trial-and-error cannot keep up with anything other than the most sedentary of environmental evolution.

It is said that Edison built 10,000 prototypes in his effort to develop a commercially viable light bulb; however, note that in his mind, he never failed, he simply "succeeded in proving that those 10,000 ways will not work". This tenaciousness is a major factor in practically all significant advances, but there was another element at work with Edison that the rat does not display, and it is much less widely recognised: the creativity that is necessary to come up with 10,000 possibilities. James Dyson demonstrated the same quality in creating over 5,000 prototypes as he sought to bring his bag-less vacuum cleaner concept to fruition.

In today's complex world the opportunity for disruption through innovation has never been greater. Shortly before I set out to write this section, there was an idea that was widely shared on the internet which powerfully highlights this point:

Uber, the world's largest taxi company, owns no vehicles.

Facebook, the world's most popular media owner, creates no content.

Alibaba, the most valuable retailer, has no inventory.

And Airbnb, the world's largest accommodation provider, owns no real estate.

The approach that allowed these companies to redefine their industries may not, in the past, have been recognised as an element of effective decision making, but the rules of the game have changed. Today, it is essential that the second approach is also taken fully into consideration: *creativity*, which we might also call *innovation* or *invention*. Any time we are faced with a novel challenge it is obvious that a new approach will need to be found.

Many of us have been so conditioned to rely on our intellectual capacity when faced with problems, that we overlook the power and importance of creativity. None of the tech success stories above arose from analysis and the desire for predictability! They came from the willingness to look beyond existing belief systems such that they could adapt to a shift of context. The forces of disruption and innovation must be embraced if decisions are to remain effective and, to do that, we must address the critical question at the start of the chapter: how can we become more creative?

The Conditions for Creativity

In referring to creativity, I'm talking about the whole process by which we come up with new ideas, and there are several factors involved that need to be understood if you are to be able to generate improvements. We've already seen one of them in the section above:

> The tenacity *to keep attention focused on the problem long enough to allow a solution to emerge.*

This is a clear, consistent trait of highly creative people, because it is rare (impossible?) that anyone arrives at a solution to a difficult challenge without having put a lot of effort into thinking about it beforehand. You are simply going to have to muddle around in it for a while. For example, Einstein thought about his general theory of relativity – described by *New Scientist* to be "one of the towering achievements of 20th-century physics" – for eight years before publishing it; and it took the Wright brothers seven years of study before they achieved their first flight.

However, there are loads of tenacious people who have no creativity whatsoever. Tenacity on its own can just as easily look like rigidity, stubbornness or even pig-headed dogmatism. The rat that gets caught out when someone alters the maze is a good metaphor for this kind of rigidity – it will hang onto its familiar solution until forced to do otherwise. The same thing could be said of Blockbuster before Netflix came on the scene, of the steel manufacturers who couldn't believe what Frederick Winslow Taylor had done, of the hot-dog eaters who never saw Takaru Kobayashi coming, and of the high jump competitors who dismissed or ignored it when Dick Fosbury first "flopped". They had all stopped questioning what they "knew" to be true.

In each of these cases, the established players were blindsided by an innovation from elsewhere, failing to respond creatively themselves because their own thinking was restricted by a combination of critical limitations that I hope you now understand well:

- Over time, they had accumulated a set of *limiting assumptions* about their operating environment.
- These had become embedded into their *conditioning*.
- This blocked them from recognising or effectively challenging their habitual thoughts and behaviours, which had become the *conventional wisdom* of the day.
- As a direct consequence they were rigid, slow to learn and were caught by surprise when the environment changed.

Creative geniuses are radically different. They can be characterised by their open, flexible and imaginative thinking, and a willingness to look beyond existing belief systems such that they can adapt to shifts of context. The decisions that enable them to leap forward aren't based on analysis and the desire for predictability. Instead they embrace uncertainty and ambiguity, deliberately seeking the opportunity that change creates. So, now we have a second vital quality required in the creative process:

The openness *to be willing to consider all sorts of possibilities, free from the constraints of conventional wisdom.*

This quality is always evident when anyone produces a creative leap – we have to stop thinking something old before we can come up with something new. For example, Swiss inventor George De Mestral had to be open enough to see something that had always been there in a new way – how difficult it could be to pull burrs from plants off his clothes after a walk – to create the possibility of his idea for the brilliant two-part clothing fastener that he called Velcro.

Neither tenacity nor openness, however, explains what happens in the actual moment when something new emerges into consciousness. This is often referred to as an insight, or an intuitive leap, and it is always evident in any genuine advance. Sometimes, many new ideas of this type will be required before a final product or solution materialises, which is why Dyson needed over 5,000 prototypes before his radical redesign of the vacuum cleaner was ready for sale. This element cannot be substituted by anything else. As such, we now have the third critical mental quality required for creativity:

A moment of insight, *in which a new solution is identified which is not a logical progression from what went before.*

Getting to Grips with Insights

It is quite possible to overlook the importance of these moments of insight because, with hindsight, the rational, intellectual mind is more than capable of taking the credit for intuitive leaps. It can be incredibly creative in finding ways to attribute them to its own ability at problem solving – as you've seen from when we looked at cognitive dissonance, and how easily we can create explanations for even huge contradictions.

To illustrate this, I'd like to take a slightly deeper look at Dick Fosbury and his now famous flop. After the event, people who believed in the supremacy of the power of the intellect wanted to believe that he had been an unrecognised genius all along, who used his mathematical knowledge as a physics and engineering student to solve the problem of crossing the bar more efficiently (his approach is mathematically superior is several ways). Not so, according to Fosbury in a 1969 interview with *Sports Illustrated*:[3]

> *"You'll read that I'm a gymnast. You'll read that I'm a physicist and that I sat down one day and figured out a better way to jump. You'll read that I ran up and tripped one day and fell backward over the bar." Shaking his head at this point, he said, "I didn't change my style. It changed inside me."*

In other words, Dick Fosbury's new technique was simply the result of an intuitive leap – it was initiated by an *inside-out process* that required no thinking or analysis.

It is notable that even Fosbury didn't really believe in his idea at first, saying in the same interview, "I wanted to be a good high jumper, and I knew I couldn't be a good high jumper backwards." Note his own limiting assumption here: even he "knew" that his new technique couldn't work. Clearly, that wasn't really knowing at all, but rather the expression of a feeling. He simply felt that it wouldn't work and, as I've been explaining since very early in the book, due to the unconscious and automatic nature of the biases and heuristics that determine how we feel, we get no warning bells relating to this sort of error: unfortunately, *when we are wrong, our internal experience is exactly the same as when we are right.*

Fosbury's problem was that, while he had had the intuition, he lacked the second quality of openness. As a result, he made what could have been a very poor decision, which would have changed the history of his sport: when practising he continued to work on improving his straddle!

It might seem almost unbelievable that, with his breakthrough there for all to see, neither Fosbury nor anyone else initially took it seriously.[4] With hindsight it all seems so obvious – but, as you know from what we covered in Chapter 1, that is the nature of hindsight. So, how it is that we ever got to see Fosbury "flop"? Well, despite his practice, he was never any good at the straddle, so he was forced to continue to use the flop in competition! It was only because he was good enough at the flop for his results with it to speak for themselves without any practice, that the old mindset was ever put to one side so that he could start to focus on developing his new technique. In other words, he hadn't cultivated openness: he got there only by necessity.

Once Fosbury let go of his old mindset, he could really get going. It was at this point that he started to focus in a scientific way on refining his approach, looking at things like the optimal run-up angles, speed, how the distance from the bar of the take-off foot needed to vary with the height of the bar. Once he'd had the idea, and recognised its value, he could then apply the third part of the formula, his tenacity – after which he soon became Olympic champion.

How many times have you fallen into the type of trap that caught Fosbury, I wonder? How many great, creative ideas have you had, that your intellect has found a way to instantly dismiss because you lacked sufficient openness to investigate their value? There is no way of knowing. Maybe they were so quiet you didn't even stop to notice them. And how many times have you experienced yourself, or others, shooting down someone else's fledgling idea before it has even had a chance to take flight?

Whenever we are faced with a problem, we always have both of the decision-making options outlined above available to us – to solve the problem by applying established formulae or understandings or by coming up with a completely new approach. The first of them is by far the easiest, and is necessary to enable us to break out of reactive mental and emotional patterns, but only creativity holds the potential to transform our results. To access it, we need the capability to step beyond the instinctive, emotional and intellectual mental functions we've already discussed and to develop the one that underpins our creative insights: our *intuition.*

Intuition: Our Fourth Mental Capability

Intuition often gets viewed with some suspicion. Perhaps this is because it is hard to know quite what it is or where it comes from, perhaps because we don't know how we know what we know, or maybe because of its connections to the psychic and paranormal. Unlike instincts, emotions and intellect, which can all be mapped onto understandings we have about relationships between brain structure and function, the source of intuition is more elusive. Whatever the reason, there are those who would like to dismiss its role in decision making completely. I believe that this is a huge mistake because, as I've tried to demonstrate, *it is the mechanism by which knowledge advances*, and that puts it at the heart of the solution to our most challenging problems.

In its favour is that, despite the fact that intuition may be hard to define, we all know, *intuitively*, what it is. That sense of "gut feel" is viscerally real, even though it may lack rational explanation. I gave some examples of intuitive awareness in the section entitled "Running on Instinct" in Chapter 1. It is the subtle knowing that takes place without having any idea why we know it, the ability to understand something instinctively, without the need for conscious reasoning, and to do so incredibly quickly.

In Chapter 4, I highlighted several articles from the *Harvard Business Review* that take highly conflicting positions on the relative importance of problem solving through rationality versus trusting intuition in the decision-making process. This kind of either/or discussion is very common. I hope I have created a strong argument for the idea that an effective approach does not involve a rigid choice, but rather the ability to flexibly find that optimal balance between the two, depending on the level of uncertainty in the external conditions. Such balance can only be achieved when we understand and use the whole brain, and all of our functions of mind, otherwise the various parts can sabotage each other, as the example of Dick Fosbury showed:

- He *intuitively* came up with a new approach to the high jump, but it conflicted with the *conventional wisdom* about the "correct" way to jump, which would have stimulated a negative feeling in the emotional brain, caused by cognitive dissonance.
- The *intellectual* brain, despite the ample evidence that he *could* do well going over backwards, reached the conclusion that the new approach couldn't work, influenced at unconscious levels by the emotions.

The solution that would have helped Fosbury was a combination of awareness of how the brain works, together with the self-awareness of how it was impacting him. Hopefully, you now have a much higher level of awareness on this subject, but we still need to look at how to drive up your self-awareness. We must get to a point where we are able to achieve balance.

Balanced Decision Making Requires a Balanced Mind and Brain

The three parts of our brain are always active, interacting with each other at levels below conscious awareness. However, as we've seen, if they are not in proper balance we'll lack the rounded perspective necessary to make reliable decisions. Some people have argued that this sort of balance is not possible, because our old, instinctive survival fears and powerful emotions have the ability to overrule the new, higher functions. However, we have been learning to solve this problem since the days of the earliest humans. Had their survival instincts been allowed to rule whenever they felt threatened, there would have been a lot of running away or bloodshed, and societies would never have been able to form or function. With the rise of the intellect, we gained the capacity for higher management of our behaviours: the only problem is that awareness of how to get better at it, much better actually, although it has been known by a few for thousands of years, is only just seeping out into the general consciousness.

Drawing together several of the factors we've looked at:

- The intellect cannot directly produce creative solutions, but it seems that we can use it to deliberately create an environment within which this can happen. Specifically:
  - maintaining the tenacity to keep attention focused on the problem long enough to allow a solution to emerge
  - developing the openness to be willing to consider all sorts of possibilities, i.e. freedom from the constraints of conventional wisdom.
- While it is never possible to make a totally rational decision, because all our decisions are influenced at subtle levels by our emotions and instincts, when the emotions take

over, our intellectual mind can struggle to maintain control, as we saw in the case of phobias:

- fMRI scans clearly show the emotional brain lighting up in even the most rational situations
- the fight-or-flight mechanism has not evolved out – evolution just added a new layer to the brain.

- Some people believe that the emotions are not to be trusted. While it may be true that without the intellectual brain to balance emotions, we lose perspective if we go too far in the other direction:

  - failure to tune into your own emotions will, over time, result in the loss of the ability to do so. This will result in weakened social skills, particularly empathy, because there's no way to recognise in others something that you aren't aware of in yourself
  - it is easy to develop the delusion that the intellect is enough, which makes people rigid and ignorant of the power of the emotions. These then show up in unconscious behaviour, often in ways that can be very damaging.

- We all routinely use numerous unconscious mental preferences and short-cuts, in the form of heuristics, habits and limiting assumptions. This happens even in the most basic day-to-day activities. Without this fast brain, everything we attempted would have to be done very slowly. But fast thinking:

  - is largely insensitive to the quality of evidence available, and provides no warning bells when it is wrong, so we need the intellectual mind to slow things down to maintain an overview of what is going on
  - cannot judge the relative merits of different ideas.

Thus, overall, it is not so much about new brain versus old brain, but rather the ability to develop the appropriate balance.

To achieve that, there are three really big topics where further answers are needed before we reach the end:

1. How can we learn to bring our different capabilities together, so that they can operate effectively across the range of potential decision-making scenarios, from *simple*, through *complicated*, into *complex*, and even into *chaos*?
2. How can we develop greater openness, to overcome habitual thinking and confirmation bias?
3. What can we say about where intuition actually comes from, and is there anything that we can do to strengthen it? And can we do anything to avoid the errors that are so common in intuitive judgments?

These questions will be the focus of Part 3.

Decision-Making Principle #7
Making decisions creatively, rather than by using a problem-solving approach, requires us to use our mind differently, learning to apply the conscious mind to the task of balancing and regulating the brain so that its different parts operate together more effectively. The key qualities of mind required are tenacity, openness and insightfulness.

Notes

1. Even at this simplified level, significant discrepancies can be found in relation to what functions are found in each layer. For our purposes, I've based my explanation on the model as presented in the book, *Super Brain*, by Dr Deepak Chopra and Rudolph E. Tanzi, Professor of Neurology at Harvard Medical School.

2. David Dunning, Kerri Johnson, Joyce Ehrlinger and Justin Kruger, "Why people fail to recognize their own incompetence" (2003) *Current Directions in Psychological Science*, 12(3): 83–87.

3. "Being Backward Gets Results", *Sports Illustrated*, 10 February 1969.

4. To experience how weird the "flop" must have looked at the time, and thereby to get some sense of why it might have been so easy to dismiss, you might find it interesting to take a look at the video of that landmark event (just search "Mexico 1968 High Jump Final" on YouTube). You'll experience how strange the old jumping technique, the Western Straddle, looks to our eyes today.

Part Three

Transforming Decision Making from the Inside Out

8

THE INSIDE-OUT CHALLENGE

"Progress is impossible without change, and those who cannot change their minds cannot change anything."

—George Bernard Shaw

If you were asked to think of a famous London taxi driver, I expect you would struggle, unless you remembered Fred Housego. He won the BBC television quiz, Mastermind, in 1980, becoming a bit of a personality in the process. One of the most notable things about Fred was that he only had one qualification when he left school. So how did he get to be so smart? Until about that same time it was almost universally accepted that the brain gets to a certain stage and then declines. But modern technology has proven that nothing could be further from the truth; the brain is like any other organ in the body: it can repair, regrow and regenerate, and that was what Fred demonstrated. As he undertook "The Knowledge" – the process of memorising London's 25,000 streets, as well as any business or landmark on them – he trained his brain to a high level of cognitive health and learned how to learn. The rest is history.

So far in this book I've identified several capabilities that are becoming progressively more important as uncertainty and volatility in the world intensify, and particularly as the impact of smart machines increases. In each case there is still a big question about "how?" to achieve them. The most important areas are:

1. The impact that our emotions have on our decision making (Chapter 4). We need to be able to overcome the way that our feelings can lead to us to become masters of self-deception, able to confirm that we are right even when we are completely wrong. **Big Question 1: How can we learn to be less controlled by our emotions, so that our observation can become more objective and we can improve our ability to see past our delusions?**

2. The need for increased levels of awareness, especially self-awareness, because increased awareness always precedes new thinking, feeling or action (Chapter 5). It is not possible to make a new choice from an old level of awareness. Therefore, in relation to personal change, we need not just awareness but self-awareness. **Big Question 2: How can we increase self-awareness?**

3. The ability to become less reactive and more responsive (Chapters 5 and 6), which requires that we become more aware of the automatic activity of the unconscious mind. We need to learn to notice the way in which we interpret things, to recognise our instinctive reactions and to process our fears differently, so that we can develop the capability to overcome habitual patterns to become more adaptable, flexible and resilient. **Big Question 3: How can we learn to see the world differently so that we can take charge of the way in which we interpret things?**

4. The need to be able to effectively balance the different capabilities of the mind and brain (Chapter 7). In particular, we must learn to manage the automatic and very fast operations of the unconscious, instinctive, emotional and intuitive mind, and the much slower processes of the conscious, rational, intellectual mind. **Big Question 4: How can our slow, conscious, mind become more capable at interrupting the flow of the very fast unconscious?**

5. The importance of becoming more tenacious, because it is the first requirement for being creative (Chapter 7). It is very hard to think of any examples where a significant advance was achieved without considerable persistence, resolve and commitment. **Big Question 5: How can we go about developing something like tenacity, which is clearly not a skill?**

6. As the second critical element in enabling greater creativity, the ability to retain an openness of mindset (Chapter 7). This moves our experiential reality such that we are more able to notice things like instances of limiting assumptions, confirmation bias or conventional wisdom (our own or those of others) for what they are, as well as enabling a greater capacity for considering new possibilities to expand thinking beyond current boundaries. **Big Question 6: Since we can't know what we don't know, how can we get better at recognising such unknowns?**

7. The ability to generate new insights by improving our ability to generate new, creative ideas, the third of the critical requirements in the creative process (Chapter 7). **Big Question 7: Is it even possible to become more intuitive and, if so, how?**

In the search for answers to the big questions highlighted above, most of the "success" literature of the last 50 years is of little help, being filled with "techniques" for growth and quick fixes. There is an obvious sort of appeal in the idea that, like the proverbial silver bullet, it is possible to quickly and easily improve personal effectiveness and relationships without undertaking the difficult work needed to change ourselves. But, like attempts to use diets to lose weight, or striving to improve one's ability to win a tough fifth set in tennis by watching the best players in the world, such approaches are close to useless until they are accompanied by change at a deeper level. You'll see in this chapter why harnessing the ability of the brain to learn in this way holds the key to the transformation of your decision making, reinforcing the key point I've highlighted from the start: that what is needed is not more knowledge, but *a mindset shift.*

Technical versus Adaptive Learning

A huge part of our challenge as we seek to develop any capability that is based on mindset, is that we are used to thinking about our personal growth in terms of skills. This is what we have been taught since our earliest days at school. It is especially true in relation to what are referred to as "hard" skills – teachable abilities that are relatively easy to measure and quantify, such as computer programming, data analysis, operation of machinery or proficiency in accounting. "Soft" skills, on the other hand, like communication (speaking, writing or listening), negotiating, teamwork or critical thinking (rationalising) are highly subjective and difficult to quantify, and much less easy to learn using the familiar approach whereby somebody who knows teaches somebody who doesn't. Yet, we still tend to make the assumption that the best way to approach them is via this old model.

Unfortunately, trying to teach mindset-based capabilities through instruction will have no greater impact than does explaining to someone that if they want to lose weight they need to eat less food, or to someone who is afraid of butterflies that this fear is illogical! A lack of understanding *isn't* the issue.

Take compulsive overeating as an example. Reward circuits in the brain start releasing feel-good hormones before eating even starts, so resisting the urge fails because the rational brain that knows it is not a good idea is weaker than the instinctive and emotional brains driving the impulse. This pattern then gets worse every time it is repeated because the behaviour becomes more deeply conditioned.

Surprising as it may seem, developing critical decision-making capabilities like tenacity, open-mindedness or intuition involves a similar neurological challenge. Hence, the traditional approach to personal development largely fails where mindset change is required, because it fails to recognise that there are two distinctly different forms of personal change which require a different type of learning, depending on which part of the brain is involved. Ronald Heifetz, co-founder of the Center for Public Leadership at Harvard University, described these two forms as follows:

- "Technical" changes, which are enabled by the development of skillsets. They have a cognitive basis, founded in the neocortex, and whilst they can be vitally important and the changes involved may not necessarily be easy, the skillsets required are well known and understood. Here, the traditional, *outside-in*, approach to learning is effective. It has an external world orientation, founded on a basic (albeit largely unconscious) assumption that we can prepare for life by learning *about* things.
- "Adaptive" changes, where there is a need to transform at a deeper level than purely to develop new skills. These changes must be addressed from the *inside out*, through a process of *realisation* and *self-discovery* rather than instruction, and involve literally rewiring the emotional and instinctive brains. Such learning impacts the way we perceive the world, our level of self-awareness, and our inner relationship with others and to life in general (more on this in the next chapter). It is not so much about what we know, but *how we know*, and for change to occur it must resonate with an inner validity that cannot be achieved when someone else tells us. This is about the transformation of mindset.

This distinction between technical and adaptive changes could not be more important as we seek to improve your decision making. To use a metaphor, imagine that the knowledge and skills we gain in life are like new applications – files and programs – being loaded onto a computer. These are the equivalent of *technical*, skill-based changes. But, over time, the operating system and underlying hardware of all computers become outdated, at which point, even though there is nothing wrong with the new applications, they won't run properly and might even slow the computer down so much that it becomes barely usable. Sometimes, it may not work at all. To enable the new applications to run properly, the computer and operating system will need to be upgraded – the equivalent of an *adaptive* change.

Similarly, with decision making, one of the biggest errors we can make is to apply technical, skills-oriented solutions to the adaptive challenges involved in creating mindset change. You could work hard on improving your rational, problem-solving capabilities, but that won't enable you to function effectively in the ambiguity of the modern age, with its requirement for us to develop a different mindset – one which gives us a much greater capacity to handle complexity. For that, you are going to need to change your brain.

Fortunately, unlike in the case of the computer where an upgrade will require new hardware, we are perfectly capable of upgrading the brain we already have!

Brains are "Plastic"

As recently as the early 1980s, brain scientists were certain that by the time we reached our early 20s, the mind (like the body) was pretty much fully developed. They "knew" that our ability to generate new mental capacity dropped off sharply post-adolescence, becoming permanently fixed around the age of 40. They believed that connections formed between the brain's nerve cells during an early "critical period" and then remained fixed in place as we aged.

Today, there is no doubt that this premise is false. The evidence to back up this statement is extensive, but I expect that you can observe it by reflecting on what you've learnt already in this book in relation to your own experience, for example:

- Have you changed the ringtone on your mobile phone and found that, for a while, you were very slow to notice it ringing? Then, quite quickly, you started to hear your calls again. What changed was that, quite literally, you developed new brain circuitry for the new ring.
- If you had always driven on one side of the road, then went abroad where the other side of the road is used, you probably found that significant concentration was required for a while in order to drive safely. But before long, driving on the other side became relatively effortless, enabled by new neural connections that created new habits in the unconscious brain.
- Have you ever sought to develop a new skill, such as playing a musical instrument, taking up a sport, or learning a language? If you improved, it was because neural real-estate had been allocated to the task in hand – you conditioned yourself to do it.

Given how obvious examples like these seem, it may be hard to understand how scientists took so long to realise that the brain could be changed in this way – a useful reminder of the power of *conventional wisdom* and *confirmation bias* to block us from seeing the obvious. Today, supported by advances in technology like fMRI scanners, there is a rapidly growing body of scientific evidence attesting to the amazing ability of the brain to respond in a highly adaptive manner to new stimuli.

Some particularly powerful examples of this type of adaptability come from studies of the visual cortex, the part of the brain responsible for processing sight. Because vision is so important to us, a huge portion of the brain is devoted to it – far more than to any of our other senses. It might be expected that this area would lie dormant in blind people but, unless they were blind from birth, it has been found that this is far from true. Scientists from the University of Tübingen found[1] that while sighted people can understand a maximum of 10 syllables per second (six syllables per second is typical when we speak), blind people's comprehension is far faster – up to 25 syllables per second. Brain scans revealed that as this was happening, part of their visual cortex was responding. Somehow, the brain must have rewired to connect parts of the brain used for hearing to those normally allocated to sight. Other work[2] has found that when sighted individuals are blindfolded, the visual cortex starts to take on completely different tasks, such as processing tactile and auditory input, and even certain linguistic and verbal memory tasks, sufficient to create measurable changes in the brain in just a matter of days.

The term now used to describe this capability of the brain to create new neural connections in response to experience is *neuroplasticity*, and it is the basis of *adaptive learning*. We now know, beyond question, that we can continue to improve our mental function in this way right through our lives, provided our brain is healthy (I remember my grandparents, post-retirement, having a race to see who could learn Russian first). Even if you have tried and failed many times, your past record is no predictor of the future, because your brain has a lifelong capacity to reorganise itself, with each new experience building on previous patterns. It is perhaps the most fundamental human capability, because it is the one upon which all our skill development is based and that gives us the ability to cope with a changing environment. In fact, as you are going to see, this type of transformation of the brain, at the level of its basic wiring, via neuroplasticity, lies at the heart of the answer to all of the big questions that I presented at the opening of this chapter.

The Power of Attention

While research has shown that there are several factors involved in triggering neuroplasticity, including environmental, hormonal and genetic influences, and exercise, there is one that stands out as being particularly useful because of its combination of power and our ability to learn to control it: our *attention.*

The ability of the brain to rewire itself based on where attention is placed, which was not discovered until the 1980s, ranks as one of the most important discoveries to date in neuroscience. In an example of one of the early studies done in this area, researchers trained monkeys to listen to and discriminate between small differences in the frequency of sequentially presented tones.[3] This stimulation was shown to lead to the auditory cortex expanding (just as your brain has to do when you change your ringtone). Similarly, if the monkeys repeatedly sensed their environment through touch, the relevant area of the brain for this capability expanded. And we now know that this is true in humans as well; for example, pianists' brains change as they refine their skills, as do those of jugglers as their coordination improves and those of aspiring London cabbies as they learn "The Knowledge".

So, where the brain is concerned, there is a simple principle: "what fires together, wires together" (and its correlate is also true: "use it or lose it!"). As we pay attention to something new, it creates new brain circuits, and as we continue to focus in the same way, it will strengthen the connections such that the physical changes in brain structure become more and more firmly established. As with exercise of the physical body, it turns out that there is a far greater risk associated with not using the brain enough than of over-using it.

There is also one further quality of attention that can be demonstrated from the research with the monkeys that were trained to listen to tones or to sense their environment through touch. Scientists also investigated what happened when they did both things simultaneously. They found that when the monkeys had been trained to focus on just one of the stimuli, only the region of the brain responsible for processing that input expanded. In other words, they could be subjected to identical stimuli – tactile stimulation and sounds – but a different result was produced, expanding a brain area or not, depending on where their attention was focused. Such work reveals a critically important building block in our journey towards improved decision making:

Attention, not what happens to us, determines how the brain becomes physically altered and which functional circuits become strengthened.

Clearly, attention is incredibly powerful. So perhaps it is not surprising that other research[4] has found better learners prioritise attention over memorisation. Furthermore, it has also been found that age is not a factor – this continues to be true for older people, who can continue to learn quickly, provided they have "really good attentive abilities".

Attention, and The Myth of "the 10,000-Hour Rule"

You may well have heard of the "10,000-hour rule". It captures the idea that this level of practice will lead to great success in any field and, perhaps not surprisingly, has been regularly repeated and is now largely accepted without question (it has become conventional wisdom ...). The first person who identified it was a psychologist named Dr Anders Ericsson from Florida State University. He observed that among violinists, the "first violin" tended to have practised 10,000 hours, the "second violin" 7,500 hours, and so on.

The problem is that this rule, which is often accepted at face value, is only half true, because part of Ericsson's finding is generally overlooked. Critically, he also said that practising for all those hours is not enough unless it is also *the right sort of practice*! This is why peak performers in practically every field have a coach (the notable exception being business, though this is also becoming much more common) who is able to look at the way they perform and give them expert feedback on their performance and what to practise next to continue to improve. Similarly, because it is difficult to see beyond our own conditioning and conventional wisdom, all of us can benefit from third-party feedback until, as self-awareness increases, our ability for accurate self-reflection and evaluation gradually increase. *The first requirement for adaptive change is to make sure that you are practising in an effective way,* which usually necessitates feedback.

In comparison with the high performers that he looked at, according to Ericsson, people who are average (by definition, most people) tend to get to a certain level of capability and then stabilise – and they typically do so after only 50 hours' practice. They lack the motivation needed to put in the effort necessary to progress.

One of my coaching clients, the MD of a sizeable business, once asked me how long it would take him to become really good at influencing others. Based on the information above, you can probably understand why my answer was: "It depends how good you want to be." The same will apply to your decision making.

Because it is not possible for anyone to immediately improve the critical enablers to creative decision making – tenacity, openness and intuition – this book cannot offer you that particular magic bullet. In fact, I'd strongly recommend that you beware of any book or course that says that it can. Because if you want to master any of these capabilities you are going to need to put in the right sort of practice, effectively targetted at those areas necessary for high-quality decision making.

Turning Development Inside Out

That final point is so important, and such a common reason why people don't progress, even when they "know" how, that I'd like to reinforce it. If you heard that a friend of yours wanted to get their physical body in shape, bought a book on how to do so, but then threw it away because they couldn't be bothered to make the exercise/lifestyle/food choices required, I'm pretty sure that I know what you would think. It would be obvious to most people that they didn't really want the change all that much, right? Likewise, if you are going to improve your decision making in a meaningful way, you'll need to be *motivated to do so*, which is the second requirement for adaptive change.

The third requirement is about the application of that motivation. *To make changes in your brain, it needs exercise.* If you want the adaptive learning necessary to improve your decision making, you will need to do what it takes – and what that means in practical terms is that you must develop an improved capacity to focus attention. I call this *intentional attention*, and it is going to take practice over time. I'll say it again – there is no silver bullet for the development of anything worthwhile, because if there was everyone would be doing it and that thing would no longer be valuable.

There are two ways that attention enables us to address those capabilities of mindset that don't respond well to traditional training and development techniques:

1. By studying new ideas with the intellectual mind, we can enable a deeper capacity for questioning ourselves. With this we can promote self-realisation and self-discovery, both of which, by providing feedback, aid adaptive learning. Helping you to achieve this goal was one of the main purposes of Part 2 of this book.

2. Direct experience, where by paying attention to inner signals we can open our awareness to include ever more of the factors that really influence our decisions. We'll be looking at this from here on in.

What these approaches have in common is their foundation in self-enquiry, which enables transformation because the learning that results is revelatory in nature. It is this that gives it enough emotional power to change the limbic brain and thereby to change choices and behaviours. In addition, learning something unexpected about ourselves in this way is the most assured way of making progress in our journey from *awareness* to *self-awareness*.

Now, as self-awareness increases, we can create an incredibly powerful, self-reinforcing, virtuous cycle, because we become better able to direct our attention consciously. To remind you of a critical concept from Chapter 5, this is possible because sensory activity is normally dealt with by the subconscious mind according to deeply buried rules. The discussion on the fight-or-flight mechanism in Chapter 6 further illustrated this principal. We saw that the way our minds scan the environment for information is based on our existing conditioning, unless we bring an intentionality to the process – the fact that they are "your" eyes does not mean that you know what they are doing! Only conscious intention can enable you to alter this automatic focus, without which you will always see what you have always seen, pretty much ensuring your ongoing entrapment by your confirmation bias. In summary:

Consciously directing attention gives us the ability to shift every aspect of our experience by shifting perceptions.

A further benefit of improved self-awareness is that, because it improves focus, it enables us to develop our capacity to recognise deeper levels of external truth. This was illustrated by the example that I gave of Susan, the turnaround executive, in Chapter 5. When we start on the inside via self-enquiry, somewhat paradoxically it enables the possibility of transformation on the outside. Conversely, the more you tend to focus on the outer world, the more you will tend to overlook the vital inner world.

To begin your journey, I recommend that you spend some time reflecting on how good you are at avoiding the "pull" of external factors. How easily do they draw your attention away from important things that you might be doing? In a world where the number of distractors is constantly increasing, and where our electronic devices are allowing so much unsolicited intrusion into our personal space from the outside, how well can you maintain your focus? These questions might help:

- When you are alerted to the arrival of a text message, email, or social media notification, how easy do you find it not to react? This is a widespread problem – some research has indicated that the average person responds to a text message in 90 seconds,[5] and over one third of business professionals say they can't leave a text unanswered for more than 10 minutes![6] If this is you, was what you were already doing really so unimportant?
- If you are in a restaurant and someone drops a plate or glass behind you that smashes, how strong is your urge to

look around? Do you look around? Do you even notice that you had a choice?

- If something has happened to upset you, to what degree do your thoughts about the event dominate your mind, and for how long? Do you find yourself stuck in a cycle where you find it difficult to regain your balance and perspective?
- When you are in conversation, how often is your attention (most likely your vision) drawn towards something happening in your environment?
- When you could (should?) be listening to someone else, how often to you find your own mind chatter dominating your thinking?
- If you close your eyes and seek to follow your breath with your attention, how long does it typically take for your mind to travel elsewhere, and how long does it take for you to realise that this has happened?

To the degree that you find yourself struggling to maintain focus in any of these situations, it indicates that you would benefit from becoming less reactive and more responsive, which requires emotional learning and growth in self-awareness. We will be addressing this in detail in the next chapter.

Overall now, extending the relationships that I've explained above to the many unconscious factors that can negatively impact our decisions, we can see that the route to a solution for overcoming them is emerging:

To improve decision making, it is necessary to learn at the level of the instinctive, emotional and intuitive minds. This can't be "instructed". It must be "constructed" intentionally.

The conscious capability that enables this learning is attention. Therefore, we need to improve our capacity for intentional attention.

This is true development, from the inside out.

A comparison of the outside-in nature of the problem-solving approach to decision making, with the inside-out approach necessary for creativity, is as follows:

Problem Solving	Creativity
Application of Logic and Rationality	Application of Awareness
Data and Fact Driven	Intuitively Led
Guided by Processes	Built on Flexibility and Openness
Requires Effort	Arises Spontaneously
Largely Conscious	Largely Unconscious
Requires Expertise	Requires Curiosity
Skillset-based	Mindset-based
Outside-In	Inside-Out

To summarise, three principles for success in adaptive learning can be seen by observing any world-class performer, whatever their discipline. They all facilitate the inside-out nature of the development work that is necessary, and they apply equally to improving your decision making:

• Some sort of *monitoring or feedback*, which can either be from others or by using your own awareness, particularly self-awareness, to recognise the quality of results that you are getting. You must have the capacity to *notice* things, especially those things you might not be expecting, to ensure that you are doing your practice in an effective way.

• *Alignment of purpose*, because purpose drives motivation. To develop mastery, you are going to have to want it. This is why, in Part 1, I attempted to highlight how the decision-making challenges that we face can be expected to change in the next few years. I hoped to increase your motivation to do the necessary work, because there is little doubt that, with the increase of artificial intelligence in the "smart machine age", it will be much more difficult to add value by adopting the old analytical, rational, *problem-solving* form of decision making. To stay relevant, you will have to get *creative*.

• Ability and competence can be improved very deliberately with *extended practice*; indeed, this is the only way to develop them. As we rehearse new ways of doing things, physiological changes take place in the brain, enabled by neuroplasticity, whereby new neural pathways can be created and become sufficiently deeply wired that they become automatic.

This understanding also provides the answer to Big Question 5: the first aspect of mindset required for creativity – tenacity – arises from the second of these points. It is simply a natural consequence of *wanting* a solution sufficiently to stay with the problem for as long as it takes to find one. Einstein summed it up: "It's not that I'm so smart, it's just that I stay with problems longer." Wanting the outcome enough itself provides the fuel required to induce this critical aspect of creativity.

Addressing "Big Questions 1 & 2"

As you know, the issue with our emotions (Big Question 1) is that they influence our decisions in many subtle ways. Any time we become emotional we lose perspective, perhaps completely, and it can seem as though the feelings are the only thing that matters. But we have all had the experience that, after the event, once we've had time to cool down, everything looks different. It is the out-of-control emotions that lead to many of our sub-optimal decisions. The starting point for overcoming this tendency towards emotionality is to learn to witness the emotions as they occur, which is a function of attention.

Similarly, self-awareness (Big Question 2) arises in the higher brain, the neocortex or intellectual brain, and is therefore also enabled by attention.

As such, it is pretty clear where we must head next – to the development of intentional attention. In the next chapter I'll seek to raise your understanding, at the level of the changes that it creates in the brain, of why attention is so powerful and how we can improve it. You'll also see why this provides us with a practical route to the development of the second and third of those qualities needed for creativity that I introduced you to in Chapter 7: greater openness and the enablement of moments of insight.

Decision-Making Principle #8
Developing the mind is an inside-out challenge, necessitating that we harness the neuroplastic nature of the brain by learning to focus attention with intention.

Notes

1. R. Douglas Fields, "Why can some blind people process speech far faster than sighted persons?", *Scientific American*, 13 December 2010.
2. For example, Lotfi B. Merabet et al., "Rapid and reversible recruitment of early visual cortex for touch", *PLOS ONE*, 27 August 2008.
3. G. H. Recanzone, C. E. Schreiner and M. M. Merzenich, "Plasticity in the frequency representation of primary auditory cortex following discrimination training in adult owl monkeys" (1993) *The Journal of Neuroscience*, 13(1): 87–10.

4. For example, work undertaken by Professor Zoe Kourtzi of Cambridge University: www.cam.ac.uk/research/features/lifelong-learning-and-the-plastic-brain.

5. http://connectmogul.com/2013/03/texting-statistics, *Connectmogul*, March 2013.

6. www.eweek.com/small-business/businesses-texting-grows-more-widespread.html, *eWeek*, 22 May 2015.

9

EVOLVING THE BRAIN

"The ability to perceive or think differently is more important than the knowledge gained."

—David Bohm

We've seen already that we are heavily conditioned to trust a problem-solving style of decision making. But to deal with the complexity, ambiguity and speed of change of the modern world, we'll need the ability to come up with creative leaps. Both anecdotal evidence and scientific research indicate that if we approach creativity with the mindset necessary for high-quality, rational thinking, we are unlikely to be successful. This is because, within the overall process required for creativity, we need that critical flash of insight – the aha! moment, when suddenly we see the problem through a different lens.

But where do intuitive leaps and insights come from, and how can we have more of them? These are vital questions for anyone wanting to continue to be a high performer in the new world. Machines already have better memories than we do, and they can perform rational processing of information much more quickly. What's more, these gaps will only continue to widen.

When you read the stories of Edison, Fosbury and other creative people, perhaps you thought to yourself something like: "Well, that isn't me. I'm just not the creative type." If so, you might be in for a surprise, because scientists are now able to observe the conditions in the brain at such times, and it turns out that there are specific things that are within our power to change and improve, both to maximise the chance of our coming up with breakthroughs and to more deeply develop this ability over time. You might be able to observe situations where you have already exhibited this insightful mindset. If you can think of a time when you solved a tricky problem, one that you had been wrestling with for a while and which involved an advancement of your previous knowledge and/or understanding, then you have already proven that you have the capability. Can you think of one? If you haven't got one yet, maybe you could just stop for a moment to remember one, then let me ask some questions:

- What were you doing when the solution came to you?
- What was your mental state at the time?
- Were you heavily focused on the task, actively trying to make a choice, or was your mind elsewhere?

I'm prepared to bet that your answer was something like, "I was relaxed ... having a shower ... taking some exercise ... half asleep at 4 a.m. ... or thinking about something else entirely." I've asked countless people these questions, and the fact that the answers are always similar is not a coincidence; it is a function of how our brain naturally operates.

It turns out that the Einsteins, Dysons and da Vincis of the world use their brains in a particular way – one that has more in common with dreaming than thinking. But much as pianos, which all have broadly the same potential, sound very different in the hands of a maestro to those of a beginner, so it is with the brain. If there were no piano virtuosos, we'd have no clue what a piano is really capable of, and without the great geniuses, we'd have a very restricted view of the creative potential of our minds and brains. This capability is also one that we can all learn and improve at; we simply need to harness the power of neuroplasticity in the right way.

Another aspect of brain operation that was covered in Chapter 7 was the need for a balanced mind and brain in decision making. It is highly significant that when I've asked that question about people's mindset at the moment of a breakthrough, no one has ever replied that they were stressed at the time. In fact, there is a very good neurological reason for that, and it stems from the fact that this mind–brain partnership only works well when we are relaxed. Let's pick up where we left off in Chapter 6, with the challenge of moving from reaction to response.

The Fundamental Question

"The most important question that we can ask ourselves is whether the inherent nature of the universe is friendly or hostile."
—Albert Einstein

That creativity requires a relaxed brain is probably unsurprising to you. The problem is simple – when we are stressed, our brain wants to handle anything that appears to be threatening as it would a survival issue, like a predator. It is not the time for learning or creativity when we are about to flee, or fight, for our life! So, irrespective of what the triggering event is, our brain tells us that we must focus on the now, not on possibility. And because this perception is related to survival, it is incredibly powerful, moving us into a state of pure reactivity. The brain then drives our behaviours highly instinctively, based on old patterns, and leaving no room for new, evolutionary, consciously selected, responses. In other words, stress forces us to focus on problems and makes it unlikely, or even impossible, that we will come up with innovative solutions.

It is hard to imagine a mindset which would be more crippling to creative decision making, and thereby to the adaptability that is becoming ever more vital. Figure 9.1 summarises the relationship

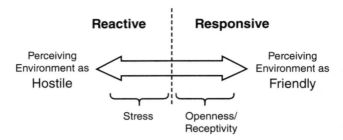

Reactive | **Responsive**

Perceiving Environment as **Hostile**

Perceiving Environment as **Friendly**

Stress | Openness/ Receptivity

Figure 9.1

between our perception of the environment (hostile or friendly), the internal mental state that this creates (stressed, or open and receptive), and the orientation towards the external world that results (reactive or responsive).

This diagram encapsulates Big Question 3: essentially, we have a continuum with maximum reactivity at one end and the maximum ability to respond at the other. If we are to become more responsive, we are going to have to shift our perceptual, and emotional, centre of gravity. Leaving out those times when you are facing a genuinely dangerous emergency, the starting point is to recognise that where you are on this spectrum is nothing more than the result of your perceptions. This was the subject of Chapter 5. For knowledge to benefit us, we must be able to make changes as a result, and to be able to cause a shift in where you are located on this spectrum requires the understanding that our interpretations of the world are not real. We are easily deceived by the activities of our own minds.

So, as I explained in Chapter 5, we can change our perception by directing attention to the largely unconscious processes that take place between our observation of something and the experience of the emotion, the goal being to identify and challenge our automatic assumptions. Carl Jung, the esteemed Swiss psychiatrist who founded analytical psychology, summed up the importance of awareness as the first stage in the process of creating personal change as follows:

> *"Until you make the unconscious conscious, it will direct your life and you will call it fate."*

The awareness that interpretation is subjective, together with the self-awareness to put it into practice, is potentially one of the most liberating ideas in this book. It can free you from having the way you feel inside dictated by what happens to you on the outside. And the key question at the heart of that is: does your unconscious perception of your environment lead you to be reactive, stuck in your old habitual patterns, or does it create openness towards possibility that allows you to respond in new ways? In relation to your decision making, and probably your life in general, I'm inclined to agree with Einstein, that this is the most fundamental question that we can ask.

Isn't Some Stress Good for Performance?

But hang on, you might be thinking, isn't it known that we need some stress for maximum performance? Certainly, this is an often-repeated piece of conventional wisdom, but does that mean it is true, particularly in relation to decision making?

The idea that some stress is beneficial is usually referenced back to the Yerkes–Dodson Law of Arousal. This states that an organism's performance can be improved if that organism is aroused in some manner, this arousal being the result of either stress or excitement. It also notes that there is a peak level of arousal, beyond which further increases result in performance *decreases.*

In support of this idea, we can readily observe three main states of action:

- *Disengagement* occurs when there is very low arousal, so we become bored, uninspired and disinterested.
- *Frazzle* occurs when demands on us become too great to handle, when the pressure feels overwhelming.
- *Flow* is recognised as the zone of optimal performance. Extensively studied because of its importance in virtually every field of endeavour, in flow, we can harness positive emotions to maximise learning, channelling them in an energised pursuit of the task at hand. This state is notable because focus is undistracted – and undistractable! – as we become totally absorbed in what we are doing. Usually, there is a spontaneous feeling of joy, even rapture.

Remember that all of these mental states are purely psychological, not a function of objective "reality", as Viktor Frankl discovered in his observation of the differing reactions of prisoners in concentration camps. Frazzle, in particular, occurs when complexity or uncertainty increases beyond what we have learnt to handle, often leading us to feel "in over our heads", which results in stress. In other words, when things feel "too complex", we are not really experiencing the complexity of the world any more than our eyes are objectively registering "what's there". We are experiencing our perception of our own inability to cope with our interpretation of what is happening.

So far, so good ... At this level, the Yerkes–Dodson Law makes perfect sense; however, and I think this is where the biggest issue lies, very often, the word arousal gets substituted for "stress", as though the two are synonymous. This kind of unexplored assumption is all too common, and potentially extremely misleading, because this interpretation changes everything.

Let's look at what is arguably one of the most outstanding performances ever, by anyone, in any discipline: the one produced by Jane Torvill and Christopher Dean at the 1984 Winter Olympics in Sarajevo. With their now-famous interpretation of Ravel's Boléro, they became the highest scoring figure skaters of all time – the only people ever to receive perfect 6.0s for artistic impression from every judge. This is how Christopher Dean describes their experience:[1]

> *"I don't think we actually saw the crowd till it was all over. We were so close, in the bubble we'd created. The fact that we were being watched by 24 million people – well, you had to put that out of your mind. We couldn't let anything get to us, not the audience, not the occasion. We'd practised every day for months. It was all about repetition. The body knew what to do."*

That is a description of focus and attention, of the ability to avoid distractions to an extraordinary degree, and of relaxation. It leaves no doubt that they were in "flow". It is not a description of stress. Steve Davis, the six times world snooker champion, summed it up beautifully when he described the challenge of playing at his best as being able, "to play as if it means nothing, when it means everything". Ask any golfer whether they hit the ball better on the range, or on the course when it "matters", and I'm fairly sure I know what the answer will be. The evidence that stress can damage performance is everywhere.

So, what is going on?

The original experiments by Yerkes and Dodson provide a good idea of where to start because they were conducted with rats, which had to navigate their way through mazes and were given electric shocks if they went the wrong way. The aim was to find out if there was an optimum level of punishment when the rats learned the quickest. They discovered that there was, and the Yerkes–Dodson "law" was born. But while this may have demonstrated that stress helps rats learn, our brain is different to that of a rat in the most fundamental and important way possible.

Introducing ... Your Frontal Lobe

In Chapter 7, I described a model of the brain called the Triune Brain, consisting of three parts: the reptilian, limbic and neocortical brains. The neocortex, if you remember, is the home of our identity, gives rise to our conscious awareness and is the enabler of all our higher human functions. Without it, you would have no awareness of your outer reality, and no ability to think, reason or plan. Without it, your senses would still communicate to you that you were cold, and you might not like it, but you would lack the ability to decide between putting on another sweater, going to a different location or turning on the heating. The part of the neocortex where all this happens is called the frontal lobe, the most critical area of which is the prefrontal cortex. It sits just behind the forehead.

Much research has shown the importance of the frontal lobe. For example, one study, which focused on decision making, observed brain operation while choices were actually being made;[2] specifically, it looked for differences depending on which of the two decision-making approaches, *problem solving* or *creativity*, was being applied. It found that when we make decisions of the problem-solving variety – using the intellect and memory in familiar environments (as we would expect to find in the *simple* and *complicated* scenarios described in Chapter 3) – the frontal lobe remains very quiet, doing little. But in situations requiring creative decision making, where we must go beyond what we already know, the frontal lobe becomes highly aroused. It is most active of all when we are faced with decisions exhibiting one or both of the following characteristics:

- There is a high level of ambiguity and no right or wrong answers, resulting in a need for lots of subjective interpretation – i.e. exactly what we face in *complex* situations
- The primary basis of the choice is dependent upon what we think we would most enjoy – i.e. there is a strong emotional component.

Such research makes it readily evident that the frontal lobe is critical to that fourth mental capability I talked about in the last chapter, *intuition*. Furthermore, it is hugely more developed in humans than any other species, with wide-ranging power, including the integration of large amounts of information and helping to coordinate and balance the firing patterns in many other areas. This role is enabled by its anatomical uniqueness – it is located in the part of the brain that connects everything else together. As such, it is essential to achieving the balanced mind and brain operation that is required for poised, well-adjusted decision making. Without it, we could not have developed any of our most advanced human capabilities.

As well as intuition and balance, other functions where scientists have discovered that the prefrontal cortex has a critical part to play in decision making include the following:

- We create conscious awareness here – when we are at our most alert and aware, this part of the brain is highly active.
- It is the seat of our self-awareness, giving us the capacity for metacognition – the power to observe our own thoughts and reflect on ourselves to assess our understanding and

performance – and thereby for emotional balance, impulse control and behavioural flexibility.

• It enables us to give meaning to our emotions and move beyond the sensory concerns of the physical world, to a model of our environment which is constructed in our mind.

• Empathy seems to arise here.

• It is the enabler of our understanding of abstract information, without which we could only plan based on concrete data.

• It enables free will and self-determination.

• From here, we make all our conscious decisions, including moral and ethical judgments.

• It gives us the ability to focus attention.

You might notice that the capabilities associated with virtually all the "big questions" identified in the last chapter are included in this list. So, what would be your opinion of anything that reduced your ability to do any one of these things, let alone something that would achieve all of them? Well, accumulating evidence is showing very clearly that that is precisely what stress does: your ability in every area listed above is diminished by stress, because of the way that it impacts the operation of the frontal lobe.

The Real Impact of Stress

Figure 9.1, depicting the reaction–response continuum, illustrates a direct consequence of what is going on in the brain. At one end, we have stress – something triggers our survival mechanism because we *perceive* a physiological or psychological threat. At the other end is the ability to respond in a flexible and adaptive manner.

We saw the impact of very high levels of stress in Chapter 6, in the example of Pete with his phobia of butterflies. In this type of situation, the amygdala, which sits in the lower brain, triggers the chemical cascade that puts the whole body on alert. Any time we are stressed like this, our eyes and brain can only focus on the external world, consumed by the threat and seeing nothing else. In this moment, even though the higher brain knows that butterflies are harmless, it has been overpowered by the false reality created by instincts, so we get overcome by the rush of fear.

The problem is that the suppression of higher brain functions originating in the prefrontal cortex doesn't only occur when stress levels are high. The very earliest experiments in this area date back to the Second World War, prompted by a need to understand why pilots who were highly skilled in peacetime made mental errors that led to crashes under the stress of battle. It was quickly discovered that exposure to even low levels of stress impaired performance on tasks that required complex, flexible thinking, but that it could improve the performance on simpler tasks where behaviour was highly conditioned. Given what we now know about the role of the prefrontal cortex, even these early studies therefore demonstrated that minor stress reduces our higher brain function. Since then, much more complex research has validated these findings.

There is now little doubt that even exposure to a mildly uncomfortable stressor will rapidly have a negative impact on our decision making – as it will on all our higher cognitive functions.

I hope I've demonstrated that we cannot make the blanket statement that some stress is beneficial; this is a great example of a limiting assumption (as covered in Chapter 2), and there are simply too many occasions when it is not true. That said, stress isn't always a bad thing; the short-term burst of extra energy and focus that gets mobilised by the release of stress hormones might help in certain situations, such as in competitive sport or if we must handle a difficult presentation at work after a night with little sleep. It can also help when performing simple, conditioned activities. But, for normal circumstances, it won't help with creative work. The hormonal changes of the fight-or-flight response are meant to be temporary, and no one can healthily sustain this state, so sooner or later the hormone rush must come to an end. When this happens, it leads to its opposite: drowsiness, loss of energy and difficulty in remaining alert and focused.

Note also that even "normal" stresses, like being stuck in traffic, can create a wide variety of physiological changes, like contributing to hypertension and coronary artery disease, impairing digestion, causing excretion of valuable nutrients, decreasing beneficial gut flora populations, decreasing your metabolism, and raising triglycerides, cholesterol, insulin and cortisol levels. Together these factors can seriously impact your health. The assertion made by highly competitive types, that they thrive on stress, doesn't bear examination at either a mental or a physical level, and may come at a high cost, resulting in impaired mental capacity and the potential for damage to their bodies.

There are still the procrastinators, however, who find that they work better when they have a deadline approaching. As the pressure to finish ramps up, it certainly seems to many of us that we become more productive. So, what could be going on here?

Procrastination is not well understood, but there is general agreement that it is linked to negative feelings – i.e. fear-related feelings at the reactive end of the react–respond spectrum. Hence, there is a need for an external motivator to get these people going! If you can think of a situation where you didn't give a task your full efforts until the deadline was looming, it is evident that you lacked the positive, internally motivated desire to see the task completed, because that would not be affected by the deadline. Lacking sufficient internal motivation, the fear acts as a psychological barrier. The approaching deadline acts as motivation to finally get started when the potential consequences of not completing the task reach the point that they are scarier than the fear that was holding us back. In this case, stress can be helpful, but only because we were already stressed. We wouldn't need it if we were already in *flow*.

The problem is, whatever its source, stress always has the same impact on higher level brain functions, setting up what looks a bit like a seesaw in the brain.

A Neural Seesaw

Under stress-free conditions, the prefrontal cortex, through its extensive connections to other brain areas, activates the release of hormones that have a positive effect on its own function, allowing even better regulation of emotions – setting up a virtuous cycle. But if something happens that causes the amygdala to trigger the release of stress hormones, these impair prefrontal cortex functioning, while reinforcing and strengthening its own – a vicious cycle. As such these two brain areas operate a little like a neural seesaw, each one having the ability to enhance itself and suppress the other. However, this is more like a seesaw where the person on one end is far heavier than the other – it is much easier for the amygdala to knock us off balance than for the prefrontal cortex to get back in charge once the amygdala has taken over, because of the amygdala's connection to survival.

Such stressors could come from unreasonable demands or deadlines, hostile colleagues, conflict with our boss, realising we've overlooked or misjudged an important task, having a disagreement with our spouse or partner, getting criticised for the way we bring up our kids or noticing a strange lump or patch of discoloured skin on our body. Whatever the trigger, internally we are still like the animal being pursued by a predator, driven by survival needs and easily overcome by emotions like anger, hatred, hostility, judgment, prejudice, blame, fear, guilt, pain, sadness and depression. Hence, once our amygdala gets triggered, it will often lead us to behave in ways that seem, on the surface, to be inappropriate, disproportionate and irrational. We look irrational because we are – we literally lose access to the rational part of our brain – which is why it is worth remembering that negative emotions can (and do) make even smart people behave as though they are stupid!

Because of its central role in generating awareness, only the intellectual brain, particularly the prefrontal cortex, can enable us to break out of such reactive patterns which are driven by the instinctive and emotional brains. Essentially, we need to increase our ability to react less and respond more, and that is going to require a shift in the way you perceive the world.

The Bad News, and the Good

Let's go back to the example of Pete and his phobia of butterflies. Theoretically, any response to a butterfly is possible, but his fearful one wins every time because he is so conditioned to give that one his attention. It feels natural, and operates without conscious involvement, triggered by the amygdala.

So why, once we recognise a pattern like that, is it so hard to change it? Over the last 20 years or so, researchers have come up with some answers on this one, discovering that not only do stress hormones impair the function of the prefrontal cortex, as mentioned above, they also cause it to literally shrink, reducing the volume of grey matter in the area. Therefore, since the prefrontal cortex is responsible for attention regulation and self-control, each time we experience stress it makes it more difficult to deal with it the next time, and so on, further intensifying the vicious cycle of out-of-control emotions.

The solution to the neural seesaw problem is simple, although it is going to require practice – it is all about our ability to control our focus of attention. In Chapter 5, I introduced the idea that attention is generally determined unconsciously ("when a pickpocket meets a saint, all he sees is pockets") and shapes our model of "reality". Next, in Chapter 6 we examined fears and phobias, to understand how anything external that we focus on will expand in our awareness. Then in Chapter 8 we extended this idea to show that, in the brain, *what fires together, wires together*: attention alone can cause the wiring of the brain itself to change. So, dealing with the seesaw requires that we develop our capacity for *intentional attention.*

Much research has been done to look at how the intentional control of attention affects the frontal lobe, including the prefrontal cortex. Given what we've covered already, you know that these are the areas associated with our capacity for intentional attention. Therefore, it would be expected that the careful focusing of attention should result in a strengthening and stabilisation of the neural networks in this area, and that is exactly what has been found to happen. Furthermore, supporting the idea that we have the potential to set up a virtuous cycle, scientists have discovered that activation levels correlate with expertise, and continue to increase with practice.

This increase in activity continues until a certain level is reached, at which point it starts to decline. This is a common occurrence associated with skill acquisition in every field: much as a proficient driver requires much less concentration to drive safely than someone with poor skills, so the expert in paying attention will achieve far higher levels of concentration while expending less effort. Similarly, if any "normal" person was to listen to, for example, a concert pianist playing the complex piano section in Beethoven's Symphony No. 8, it is almost certain that they wouldn't notice any mistakes, while the virtuoso pianist would do so effortlessly, recognising even the smallest of errors. Scientifically, we all experience the same thing – pressure waves in the air striking the eardrum – but through tens of thousands of hours of practice, the expert's mind can do much more with that information. In other words, attention dramatically shifts the level of awareness in the area to which the expert has attended. Exactly the same thing happens in the frontal lobe as we practise – the effort required to sustain attention will reduce over time, while we simultaneously become better at all of those capabilities supported by that part of the brain.

So, the good news here is very good: if you are willing to learn how to focus attention on the frontal lobe, and practise it, you will create changes in the prefrontal cortex that have the potential to transform not only your decision-making capabilities, but many other higher cognitive functions as well.

And finally, what of the impact on the amygdala of this kind of focused attention on the frontal lobe? If the principles of the neural seesaw and neuroplasticity are correct, then if we practise intentional attention it should lead to decreases of both amygdala activity and brain tissue in that area, which would be experienced as a reduction in stress by anyone concerned. And this is exactly what studies have found. For example, researchers found[3] that just eight weeks of practising deliberate attention for only 20 minutes per day (on average) resulted in reductions in perceived stress among the participants which correlated positively with decreases in the density of brain tissue in the amygdala. The more stress decreased, the greater was the reduction in density. For many people, this will be the most rapid and easily observable benefit if they start to work on improving their *intentional attention.*

From Reaction to Response: Shifting Our Perceptual Centre of Gravity

"All things are subject to interpretation. Whichever interpretation prevails at a given time is a function of power and not truth."
—Friedrich Nietzsche

Through this mechanism of consciously focusing attention, we literally gain the ability to shift every aspect of our experience from the inside out. It enables us to change our perception of "reality", because as the brain rewires we will move away from the reactive end of the reaction–response continuum, gradually experiencing the environment as less hostile and more friendly. This is essential for creativity because, as we've explored in detail, there is no room for anything new when our survival instincts have been triggered. With this perceptual shift, we will address all of the first four Big Questions from the previous chapter.

In principle, such a change is not hard to achieve: we need to learn to slow down enough that we can engage the thinker, to deliberately introduce a pause between any external trigger and when we start to act to handle it. Breathing offers a remarkably powerful way, probably the simplest one I know, by which we can centre ourselves enough to do this. Research has shown that it can take as little as five seconds of conscious, deep breathing to short-circuit the "neural highjack" which occurs when the threat response is triggered. If you can stay with it a little longer, just 20 seconds has been found to allow the brain to reorganise itself and for there to be an increase in activity in the frontal lobe. As you now know, this will then automatically improve attention, emotion regulation and decision making, so as you do this you will become better able to find a more adaptive, appropriate and evolutionary solution to whatever problem you are facing.

You can use this approach either when you've already been trig-gered and are experiencing a negative emotion, or at any other time throughout the day when you want to become more cen-tred, and it's brilliant because you can do it without anyone else noticing. Here is one effective method:

1. Take your attention off whatever is happening in your environment.

2. Focus on your breath and take between one and three deep, conscious breaths (more is great if you have time, but only one is required!). It is more effective if you can breathe from your diaphragm (i.e. pulling the air right down into the tummy region) and notice the sensation of the air moving into and out of your lungs. Take at least 4 to 5 seconds on the in-breath and around 5 to 10 seconds on the out-breath, breathing quietly and naturally through the nose.

3. As you breathe, allow your body to relax. Take the time to focus on how it feels to have your lungs fill and then empty. If appropriate, it may help to also allow your eyes to close for a few moments.

Why not try it now? See if you can notice the changes taking place in your body as you breathe in this way, giving it a chance to relax. In fact, the benefit we can get from this comes from more than just attention, as research is increasingly showing that the way we breathe – fast and shallow when stressed or slow and deep when relaxed – affects mood, stress levels and even the immune system.

Becoming Mindful

What this type of breathing practice will do is to bring you more fully into the present moment, and it is a very simple way of approaching what is commonly these days being called mindfulness. For some people, as soon as mindfulness is mentioned they think religion, but it really has nothing whatsoever to do with religion, though it has been practised by some of them since ancient times.

There are lots of definitions of mindfulness, such as this one from Jon Kabat-Zin, one of the people most credited with introducing mindfulness to the West: "Mindfulness means paying attention in a particular way: on purpose, in the present moment, and non-judgmentally." But rather than get caught up in individual definitions, which operate at the level of knowing, my advice is that you seek to understand what is implied by them, to recognise the feeling, and to understand how you can put it into practice.

My perspective on this is that mindfulness is about being mentally calm, relaxed, open, accepting, fully present and non-judgmental. It implies a level of awareness whereby attention can be focused in a very stable way, not easily getting pulled off by distractions. In this state, the intensity of thinking is greatly diminished, and we will experience the information from our senses in real time. This helps us to become much more flexible in the way we respond to the world, being less restricted by habits, expectations, assumptions or previous experiences. It gives us the ability to *notice our experience*, and thereby creates the possibility of making changes when it is beneficial to do so. It doesn't sound so mystical put like that, does it, because isn't that the same language we've been using to describe what happens when we activate the frontal lobe? It shouldn't, because it is.

Unfortunately, much research has discovered that the normal human state could more accurately be described as mindlessness, and it is so natural and automatic that it is often referred to as the *default* mode. It becomes active when nothing much is happening, or when thinking is directed at the past or the future. In this state, we are highly reactive to our automatic interpretations of what is happening, which has the result that we experience our thoughts as being true, getting heavily locked into habitual behaviours. This network is active most of the time while we are awake, but it can be hard to recognise what is happening because it takes so little effort for the brain to operate this way.

When we can notice our experience through mindfulness, we can take in more external and internal information, because we are moving away from the survival emotions that lead to very narrow focus, and see more options. Each time you practise becoming more mindful, for example with the breath exercise above, you will get better at noticing the shift in the other direction as it happens. When you can observe yourself with this level of self-awareness, you will be able to break out of reactivity, enabling you to:

- become progressively more aware of how you are processing your experience, and over time this will greatly improve your ability to *pay attention with intention*
- get closer to the "reality" of an event, perceiving it more accurately and therefore being able to make much more appropriate choices about how to respond
- improve your ability to generate the sort of high quality feedback that I highlighted earlier as being necessary for the limbic brain to learn effectively.

These changes will all tend to facilitate better decision making, and the foundation is improved mindfulness. In the next chapter, therefore, we'll look at the application of mindfulness to the key remaining qualities of creative decision making: openness and insightfulness (tenacity having been addressed in Chapter 8), and I'll also help you to understand where to start if you want to improve your own mindfulness.

Decision-Making Principle #9
As we practise intentional attention, we can predictably and reliably evolve our brain to reduce reactivity and become more responsive, flexible and adaptive.

Notes

1. Christopher Dean and Jayne Torvill, "How we made Boléro", *The Guardian*, 22 April 2014.
2. Elkhonon Goldberg, *The Executive Brain: Frontal Lobes and the Civilized Mind*, Oxford University Press, 2001.
3. B. K. Holzel, J. Carmody, K. C. Evans, E. A. Hoge, J. A. Dusek, L. Morgan, R. K. Pitman and S. W. Lazar, "Stress reduction correlates with structural changes in the amygdala", (2010) *Social Cognitive and Affective Neuroscience*, 5(1): 11-7.

10

UNLOCKING CREATIVITY THROUGH MINDFULNESS

"My experience is what I agree to attend to. Only those items which I notice shape my mind – without selective interest, experience is an utter chaos."

—William James

William James, who has been labelled by some as the "father of American psychology", powerfully captures the difference between being mindful and mindless – his warning being that without attention, the way we experience life will be "utter chaos"! I hope that I've demonstrated the value of mindfulness – the ability to pay attention in a deliberate way – and that this is especially true in a changing environment, through the many examples I've offered. Because of the importance of attention to our ability to learn, I believe that we can go as far as to say that we can only afford to be mindless under two conditions: we know everything, or nothing is changing. As the speed of change increases, therefore, mindlessness will come at an increasingly high cost.

The following bullets highlight the key points from the discussion over the last two chapters, as they relate to mindfulness. They make it evident why we can be confident that becoming more mindful will allow us to address many of the challenges of creative decision making addressed in this book:

- The highest levels of performance occur in a state which is often called "flow", or "being in the zone": when we feel completely absorbed in an activity, with strong but effortless concentration from an open, relaxed mind.
- Stress diminishes performance in creative tasks because, by putting us into our fight-or-flight mode, it limits (or shuts off) access to our higher cognitive functions.
- Stress also literally shrinks the frontal lobe, making it harder and harder to stay balanced the longer it lasts.
- The solution is that we must learn to slow down enough to re-engage the thinker, so that we can observe ourselves with self-awareness, allowing the frontal lobe to regain control.
- We can strengthen the frontal lobe simply by deliberately focusing our attention and, like a muscle, each time we do so this brain area, because it is responsible for attention, will develop.
- As we do so, our fight-or-flight mechanism will start to lose its power, eventually allowing the intellectual brain to override even the most instinctual fears, such as the startle response.
- Focusing attention is something over which we can exercise the power of intention, so we can literally use our mind to evolve our brain.
- Through intentional attention, we can then learn to access more of our creative capabilities and develop a mindset that will allow better performance, more of the time.

Overall, this summarises a scientifically validated process for training the brain to work better – by focusing attention to improve mindfulness.

Achieving Optimal Performance

Simple exercises, such as the one I outlined in the last chapter, using the breath to become more present, definitely help to improve mindfulness, especially at times when we find ourselves being pulled into reactivity. However, if you want to become highly competent in this area, you'll need to be much more deliberate about it, just as you would need to do to develop any other capability.

Do you remember that way back in Chapter 1, in the section entitled "Accessing More of Our Potential", I questioned whether we can learn to deliberately tap into our enormous unconscious capabilities, evidenced through our heuristics, in a deliberate way that would help our decision making? I was categoric, even back then, that we can.

The basis of the approach needed to achieve this is the same as the one they discovered, during World War II, to teach aircraft recognition. For that matter, it is also what's necessary to improve at playing a musical instrument, hitting a golf ball, learning a foreign language or discerning the subtle differences between wines. In every one of these cases, we can see in action the principles of adaptive learning that we covered in Chapter 8: motivation, feedback and extended practice. Motivation provides the interest levels necessary to try something, to take feedback and learn from it, then to apply that learning in practice (through trial and error) to generate improvements and gain more feedback. And so it goes on. Another way of saying this is that we give the subject that we are attempting to learn our focused attention, and when we do so, the result is the development of a skill.

Now, here is the critical point...

If you think of any master when they are "performing" their art, can you recognise that they are always extremely mindful? Think of the wine expert who is about to taste a wine. Don't they always pause and focus deliberately on what they are about to do? They may well close their eyes, withdrawing from their other senses to cut out distractions, to allow as much brain capacity as possible to be devoted to noticing the taste. If you picture Jonny Wilkinson, the former English rugby union player who at one time held the record as the highest international points scorer, as he prepared to take a penalty kick, you can see the same thing. Picture Torvill and Dean when they were performing the Boléro in Sarajevo, or musicians during a concert, or athletes practising their well-rehearsed warm-up or pre-shot routines. They all display a huge focus on what they are doing right now. They all know, consciously or unconsciously, how to access the state of flow: the positive mood and present moment, relaxed, open awareness that enables us to be aware of distractions without being distracted by them. This state is synonymous with mindfulness, and it is built on the ability to pay attention with intention.

Furthermore, as covered in the last chapter, this flow state is impossible to achieve when our threat response has been triggered, which is why I believe Einstein was right to suggest that the most important question we can ask ourselves relates to whether we see the world as friendly or hostile. Intentional attention also offers the solution here, because when applied in a particular way it reduces reactivity and improves higher cognitive capabilities. In this mindful state, we can then be much more flexible and adaptive.

Finally, as we also observed in the last chapter, by practising focusing attention with intention, the very act itself strengthens the part of the brain that enables that focus – setting up the ultimate virtuous cycle. As such we can see that the ability to pay attention is actually a skill, and once it is well developed it is expressed as mindfulness.

The Ultimate Skill

"Understanding and managing attention is now the single most important determinant of business success."
—Tom Davenport, former director of Accenture
Institute of Strategic Change

Clearly, high performance requires a high level of mindfulness, which is both underpinned by intentional attention and impossible without it. This is because attention is:

- essential to effective learning
- the key to achieving the state of "flow" that is so key to optimal performance
- capable of rewiring the brain at the deepest levels
- self-reinforcing, so that the better we get, the better we'll get.

I expect you can now see why I suggested, in Chapter 7, that the ability to improve our level of intentional attention is the ultimate skill – it is the basis of our ability to condition ourselves to master anything. Like all skills, it requires practice, and in this case that practice is usually called meditation.

In the last chapter I clarified that mindfulness has nothing to do with religion. Sadly, my experience is that this association is made even more strongly when meditation gets mentioned. I say sadly, because this can result in people who have some form of dislike of religion dismissing meditation by association. I've spent a long time building up to this point, because I wanted to build a solid, scientific, logical case prior to risking triggering this reaction. While there are many ways in which it is practised, the word "meditation" is just a label, referring to a form of mind training based on deliberate attention. Where I've used terms such as "focused attention" earlier in this book, in most cases they could have been substituted with "meditation". So, if you have felt a negative reaction, can you notice it and think what you would do if you could choose to respond instead?

There's nothing mystical or weird about meditation. Whatever form it takes, it is skill training, pure and simple, in the skill of being able to pay *intentional attention*. Like going to the gym, if you are willing to put in the effort, you'll benefit, but if you just get yourself a couple of guided meditation apps, and perhaps some books, or attend a course, then dabble around in it for a while before returning to your busy life, well...

Why am I highlighting this again? Because my experience is that most people know about meditation and mindfulness these days, and many have an app or two, or some books, and they may have even given it a go, yet few have a regular practice. There are various reasons why this happens, these being the big ones:

- They don't believe that meditation can help them, either because they aren't aware of its benefits or because they feel that they are already sufficiently well balanced and focused.
- They believe in the benefits, but still lack the motivation. This is understandable, because who isn't busy these days, and it is essentially a question of values – it means they believe that spending their time in another way offers greater benefits to their life.
- They can't sit still, with their eyes closed, in a quiet place, and follow their breathing, because they hate the experience. Their life must be busy all the time, and spending time being quiet, with themselves, is impossible. I've had some very senior and successful clients like this, and it is a big warning.

If you don't already have a regular meditation practice, does one of these apply to you? Perhaps you can notice that the information that I've already presented is shifting your level of motivation?

Getting Present

"All of humanity's problems stem from man's inability to sit quietly in a room alone."

—Blaise Pascal, 18th-century
French philosopher and mathematician

You could try this right now. Find a comfortable seated position, relaxed and alert, with your spine erect and (preferably) unsupported, and feel as though you have a thread gently pulling upwards through the top of your head. This posture will help you to maintain a relaxed and alert state. Now, close your eyes and notice your breathing. As in the exercise in the last chapter, I recommend following the breath in the body, but if it is easier for you in the nostrils, that is okay as well. Don't try to change the breath – just watch it, and feel the sensations that it creates. If fact, don't try to "do" anything. It is one of the biggest misunderstandings of meditation – and one that I believe may be responsible for a lot of people giving up, because it guarantees failure – that we should try to empty our minds. Much more instruction is possible, of course, but for now, just keep your attention on your breath as best you can, gently returning it back there each time you find that it has wandered. Five minutes should be enough.

How did you get on? That was a mini-meditation. It is conceptually very simple, isn't it? But unless you already have a regular meditation practice, you probably discovered that it is not so simple in practice. If so, you've just experienced the way that *outside-in* instruction can disguise a truth that is revealed quickly and easily by *inside-out* self-discovery. If you haven't tried it yet, why not? You can't really learn this stuff outside in – before you can possibly "know" it, you'll need to embody it from the inside out. If you gave it a go, how often did your mind drift off, and how long did it take for you to realise when that had happened? During this exercise, how much were you talking to yourself? What were you saying? How comfortable or uncomfortable was it? And what does all of the above tell you about your current ability to direct attention with intention?

And what about the discomfort I highlighted in the previous section, when people can't just sit and be still? Do people really hate the experience, as I've suggested and, if so, why would this be a big warning?

One study that looked at this area wired people up so that they could push a button and give themselves electric shocks, then asked them to sit quietly with no distractions for 15 minutes.[1] Even though every one of the participants had previously stated that they would pay money to avoid being shocked, two thirds of men and a quarter of women zapped themselves in preference to being alone with their thoughts (guys, in particular, this is worth a deeper look!). By inference, presumably these people would therefore pay money to avoid meditating!

Given this awareness, it seems unsurprising that so many people choose not to meditate (one poor guy pressed his button 190 times in 15 minutes – imagine living in his mind!). There has been some suggestion that this behaviour is the result of boredom, but I think that is doubtful. I believe that it is much more likely to be a sign that they are simply stressed out, because the less willing we are to direct attention inside, the more it indicates that we feel there is danger in the external world. As we covered in Chapter 6, it's an automatic survival response: no one is going to be able to sit in contemplation when they feel as though a predator is about to eat them. What this means is that, unfortunately, those who find it the most difficult to meditate are probably the ones who would get the most benefit. Furthermore, since flow/optimal performance depends on the absence of stress, then if you can't sit and focus internally it is a good indicator that you are operating below your potential.

So, how does meditation help? Focusing in this way works to build mindfulness because the sensations of the breath can only be felt in the present, whereas worries, fears, doubts, regrets, grievances and grudges all exist only in a picture of the past or future that is created in the mind. None of them are facts, but that doesn't mean they don't have the power to dominate attention. Now, as we already know from the last chapter, mindfully focusing attention strengthens the prefrontal cortex and weakens the amygdala, so the practice will automatically shift your perception so that the world appears friendlier. In terms of your experience:

- As you learn to focus attention, you'll become more and more observant of what is going on in the mind. Using the breath as a focus provides an essential reference point, because without a central focus to be distracted from it would be very difficult to recognise distraction for what it is, and thereby to notice the mind wandering.
- Noticing more will create a sense of detachment from thoughts and emotions, which you'll see constantly shifting without any input from you, and that will change your relationship with the emotions.
- At that point, you'll start to generate enormously more self-awareness, which is the starting point for change. You won't feel the same "grasping" of those inner experiences you like and judgment of those you don't, allowing your mind to calm down and your reactivity to diminish.
- Now, you'll be able to make a conscious choice instead, and that means you can respond rather than reacting.

- Thus, as you cultivate your present moment awareness, you will experience your mind as being less cluttered and full of distractions, giving you more resources to focus on the task in hand in an adaptable and flexible manner.

As we progress I'll give further examples of scientific research that evidences the benefits of meditation as they apply specifically to openness and intuition. We'll start with openness, because I want to contrast what happens when attention is not intentional with the mindful awareness I've just described, and show how the inability to handle distractions will cripple your decision making.

Attention in the Absence of Mindfulness

In Chapter 5 we looked at why the mental quality often called "open-mindedness" is not really possible to achieve, because we automatically bring our own biases into the way we perceive and evaluate everything. Furthermore, as you know from Chapter 6, the reactive focus precipitated by our fight-or-flight mechanism is extremely limiting, because it narrows our focus to include only those things the mind considers to be directly relevant to survival. Both factors have a huge impact on decision making, making it difficult or impossible to ensure that we have properly considered the options and are not making a disastrous error. But what about when we just become very absorbed in a task, such as solving a problem? Can this lead to us failing to consider vital information?

My childhood home had a steep driveway, sloping up to the road. Dad was going cycling, and had attached his bike to the roof of his car to take it to the start-point, but it was very icy that day and he couldn't get traction to move backward up the drive. Thankfully, there was an easy solution: to roll forward into the garage so that he could get up some momentum before hitting the ice. But it didn't take long to realise what a very poor decision this was – as soon as he rolled the car forward we got unmissable feedback to help us to learn! Unfortunately, the bike didn't fit …

Looking back, it seems like I was wondering how I'd been so stupid even before the bike had hit the ground. It was impossible to imagine how we'd both managed to miss something so obvious. Indeed, I'd fully understand if you are wondering exactly the same thing right now! Let's face it, I was standing right beside the car and could clearly see that the top of the bike was much higher than the garage door. But things often take on a new clarity with hindsight, as we saw in Chapter 1. Furthermore, we all do things that seem stupid after the event from time to time, don't we? So, what on earth is going on?

A great example of the problem of failing to "see" a situation clearly, that you may well already be aware of, is the popular "invisible gorilla" video (if you haven't seen it, and want to, you'll need to do so right now, before I spoil the punchline). Originally created as part of an experiment conducted at Harvard University, it is of two teams of basketball players. Viewers are invited to count the number of passes made by one of the teams, unaware that, in the middle of all the activity, a person in a gorilla suit will walk through the group. Despite how obvious the gorilla is to anyone who already knows about it, scientists have discovered that most people miss the gorilla the first time they watch it, and in other, similar, experiments this number can be as high as 80%. What makes this particularly interesting is that, without the task of counting the passes, pretty much everyone will see the gorilla. So, it must be the focus on the task of counting that causes us to miss what would otherwise be obvious.

The name given to this mental tendency is inattention blindness, and it is thought to be the result of natural limits to how much we can attend to: when focusing on one task, such as counting passes, it is hard to notice much else.

This experiment is highly representative of life: there are always multiple objects or streams of thought that we could concentrate on, and if we become locked onto any one of them it will dominate our attention, leading to us becoming unaware of other things around us.

Now, combine that understanding with what we learned from the monkeys that were conditioned to focus on a particular stressor – either a tone or a tactile stimulus. Once conditioned, even if they were exposed to both stressors, they would only be aware of the one they had been trained to notice. The implication here is huge:

The thing that gets our attention is not necessarily that which is most important, or beneficial, because our focus is so heavily driven by conditioning.

At its most extreme, as we've seen, the unconscious nature of our conditioning results in phobias, but the same effect is at work at all other times, narrowing our focus and potentially hiding things that might be right in front of us, even when they are extremely important. Quite literally, when we are not aware of something because we are focused elsewhere, it ceases to exist for us in that moment and therefore cannot be considered in our decision making. Think about it – did your left little toe exist for you before I mentioned it? Did your right ear? Did the feeling of your clothing against your skin? As William James said, our experience is shaped by our attention, and, as I highlighted in Chapter 1, we get no warning bells when our focus is leading to an error.

I probably spent 25 years thinking I'd been incredibly stupid the day I allowed my dad to drive forward into our garage with the bike still on the roof. Now, I realise that I was just being human (phew!): it was simply that my attention wasn't on the bike because the problem of the ice had led us both to become overly focused elsewhere. The actual problem was a lack of openness, which blocked awareness to such an extent that even critical, and obvious, information outside the area of attention was completely missed. Hopefully, if this kind of incident happens to you, now you know this you won't have to spend as long questioning your own intelligence as I did that time.

Bounded Awareness

"Today's advanced knowledge is tomorrow's ignorance."
—Peter Drucker

Our tendency to routinely overlook highly relevant, easily accessible, and readily perceivable information during the decision-making process is well established; it has become known as "bounded awareness". Over-focusing is a significant part of the problem, but by no means all of it because, in addition, we are also quite likely to miss things that …

- we are not expecting
- we have never experienced before
- don't happen very often
- change very slowly
- are routine aspects of our environment that we have learnt to take for granted.

I've referred to several practical examples related to bounded awareness earlier in the book – including the case studies of the Challenger space shuttle disaster, Frederick Winslow Taylor, Takaru Kobayashi and Dick Fosbury – where problems or opportunities existed but most people literally couldn't see them. It is obviously very difficult to accurately assess the "facts", no matter how critical it might be to our desired outcome or how "intelligent" we are. Thus, with incomplete awareness, we will inevitably place false boundaries around the situation, which can make it difficult or impossible to recognise what we don't know, or to innovate. Such boundaries affect every part of the decision-making process, causing us to fail to:

- see or seek out key information needed to make a sound decision, while seeing other equally accessible and perceivable information
- use the information that we are aware of because we don't recognise its relevance
- share important information with others, thereby limiting their ability to fully contribute to the process.

Just as the task of counting passes in the "invisible gorilla" video increased the likelihood that people would miss the gorilla, these tendencies all increase the more intensely we focus on any individual aspect of our environment, because focus without mindfulness narrows attention.

The other situation that creates major limitations of awareness is when we are motivated in favour of a particular outcome. The associated emotions then affect our objectivity through *cognitive dissonance*, *motivated reasoning* and *confirmation bias* (see Chapter 4), making it very difficult for us to become aware of any information that is inconsistent with our preferred viewpoint. In these circumstances, our perception may bear little relationship to "truth", being shaped instead by our own biases and inner desire for comfort. The irony of it all is inescapable:

Just when we most need another viewpoint ...

just when it is most important that we see things more objectively ...

because our prejudices, biases and fears are heavily distorting our experience ...

is precisely when we become the most rigidly attached to our existing beliefs!

Clearly, the openness we are seeking in order to enable creative decision making is impossible when we are trapped in bounded awareness. So, what is the solution? How can we address the problem of bounded awareness to more "accurately" perceive the stimuli available to us and improve the reliability of our decision making? I recommend two powerful solutions:

1. **Seeking to disprove** what you believe. This is superficially an *outside-in* approach, but note that it must be enabled by sufficient *self-awareness* to realise that you may be missing something, which is an *inside-out* capability.

2. **Meditation to improve intentional attention**, enabling you to notice more. This is inherently adaptive in nature and can only be achieved through *inside-out* development.

Seeking to Disprove

"Great doubts, deep wisdom. Small doubts, little wisdom."
—Chinese proverb

Let's start with a safe assumption: we are going to be wrong a lot in life and, often, the illusion of knowledge can be far more dangerous than ignorance because of the way it narrows our thinking. Next, we have a simple fact: our capacity to believe we are right even when we are completely wrong is practically limitless, because we live in a conceptual world that we created. Introspection easily reveals both things to be true, and the reason is that what we call "reality" is not something objective that we perceive – it is purely subjective, created in our mind.

The issue is that when we "know", we can't learn, we can't be creative and, like the coaches watching Dick Fosbury flopping, we'll most likely miss the truth even if it is right in front of our eyes. We've seen, for example, that our *confirmation bias* is so robust that we can find information to justify our beliefs even when disconfirming or falsifying information would be more useful.

That being the case, doesn't it make sense, with any important decision, to test it, thoroughly, from the starting assumption that we might be wrong?

The tragedy of the Challenger space shuttle disaster that morning in January 1986 clearly demonstrates the importance of the start point. There seems little doubt that the executives responsible for the decision wanted the mission to take place and began with the assumption that it would be safe to do so. During the tele-conference when the decision was made, Morton Thiokol's vice president of engineering, Bob Lund, who was responsible for the maintenance of the SRBs, said that his team felt that the flight would not be safe, because of the temperatures that day; how-ever, he could not "prove" their concerns were valid,[2] and his data was dismissed as inconclusive. How different might it have been had they set out to find proof that it was safe, rather than that it wasn't?

There's nothing novel in the suggestion of looking for discon-firming evidence. This principle is the basis of scientific thinking, because it forces a rational evaluation of ideas, allowing the sub-jectivity of personal opinions and the biasing effect of emotions to be minimised – it puts the intellectual brain back in charge. In science, the more effort that has been put into disproving a theory without success, the stronger the theory becomes. The same thing will happen to your confidence in your own decisions if you rig-orously challenge them, because as you seek to disprove, deeper "levels of truth" will open to you.

This is primarily a question of learning to welcome alternative per-spectives, proactively seeking evidence that flies in the face of what you currently believe and recognising that any attachment to an outcome, or to a pet idea, will likely block you from mov-ing closer to the truth. The power of doing so was highlighted in the study by Philip Tetlock that I described in Chapter 3 – the one with the conclusion that the average expert "is not much better at predicting the future than a dart-throwing chimpanzee". There were some findings in that study that are highly relevant here:

- People with some knowledge did better than those who knew nothing.
- But the experts with the most knowledge were often the least reliable and the most resistant to admitting it when they were wrong.
- Only one thinking style aided prediction: considering multiple explanations and balancing them together.

So, we have a clear challenge: the more expertise we develop, the more likely we are to become overconfident that we are right, becoming constrained by our own belief in our ideas. Generalists, on the other hand, who rely on broad knowledge, are much more psychologically receptive to ideas which differ from their own and tend to be much more aware of how much they might not know. These people are much better at improvising and adapting.

There is very little for you to "do" here, other than to be willing to be more open. The biggest problem to be addressed is that we easily become closed, and rigid, without even realising it. There are several indicators that might help you to recognise that you've closed down, including:

- not having, or being unable to see, any contradictory evidence
- believing that you don't need to test your ideas because you just "know"
- dismissing an idea because it is new and unfamiliar, or unproven
- getting annoyed by alternative perspectives or finding it difficult to listen to the ideas of people who disagree with you
- deciding on the merits of other people's ideas before they even finish speaking.

I strongly urge you to keep in mind that *having a feeling of certainty that you are right is absolutely no guarantee that you are*, which can be enormously helpful in maintaining openness. If you can listen to others with a willingness to be influenced, being open to the possibility that you don't know (even when you feel certain you do), and act in the knowledge that there are lots of things that you don't know you don't know, you will learn more and overlook less. For certain, this will considerably open the boundaries of your awareness.

Meditation Improves Attention

A second approach to reducing the impact of bounded awareness is to develop your ability to focus attention deliberately. We've already seen that the mind has a limited capacity for attention, which results in things we are not focused on being overlooked. Whether they are important at a rational level can be completely invisible to us in our evaluation, because focus is usually driven unconsciously.

Obviously, many times our oversights don't matter, but what if you are driving, and your attention is drawn to a pedestrian who almost stepped out in front of you. Now, what is the chance you'll notice the cyclist pulling out from the upcoming side-street? Even when we've established that the pedestrian doesn't present a hazard, scientists have found that there will be a short period after our observation of the first event in which we have a blind spot in our attention: they call it attentional blink.

To measure attentional blink, scientists ask participants to look for two targets, such as the pictures of two dogs shown in a series of pictures of cats. What they find is that if the dogs are shown too closely together, people don't see the second one, and by varying the time between the targets they can measure the length of the "blink". They've found that it typically lasts for half a second and, unfortunately, it means that for that period you won't be able to see that cyclist.

The attentional blink was at one time thought to be a fixed property of the nervous system, but studies have shown that it can change with practice – we'd expect this, of course, from what we know about neuroplasticity. An example of such a study was led by Richard Davidson, a professor of psychology and psychiatry at the University of Wisconsin. In it, the attention levels of people who had trained in meditation for three months were compared with novice meditators.[3] In this case, he used two numbers embedded in a series of letters, and found that everyone could detect the first number, but recordings of brain activity showed that the less-experienced meditators stayed focused on the first number for longer, and so they missed the second one. Those with more experience were able to shift their attention more easily, as if letting the first number go, increasing their ability to detect a second target within the half-second time window. Thus, we can see an important paradox:

As we learn to focus attention in a mindful way, it reduces the likelihood that we become overly focused, increasing our openness and flexibility (addressing Big Question 6).

One other important finding was that, though the ability to see the first target did not change with meditation, the amount of brain activity required to do so was significantly reduced. Furthermore, the size of the decrease strongly predicted their ability to detect the second target. This proves the key premise of the last chapter, that:

Attention is a flexible, trainable skill.

This experiment also provides evidence for a couple more very important conclusions. First, there is often a debate about whether the benefits of meditation are limited to when it is being practised, or become a trait enabling improved attentional abilities that last outside the period of meditation. Because the subjects were not meditating during the test, their improvement provides evidence that this kind of mental training does cause lasting changes in how people allocate their mental resources – as we would expect from our knowledge of neuroplasticity. Second, since it shows that practice reduces the effort involved in paying attention, the attentional blink experiment also suggests that meditation might help us to achieve the calm, relaxed state necessary to get into "flow"; and that is indeed what has been found to happen. This relaxation effect of meditation is transformational in many ways, and I'll say more about this shortly, when we look at developing intuition.

Just one more thing, before we move on, because I'm guessing you may be concerned you don't have three months to go on a meditation retreat. Thankfully, many studies have found that results can be achieved much more quickly than that. At the other end of the spectrum, one study[4] demonstrated that just 20 minutes of meditation instruction per day for five days resulted in significant improvements in participants' levels of attention compared to a control group, as well as delivering many other benefits such as lower anxiety, depression, anger and fatigue, decreases in stress-related cortisol and an increased immune response. Typically, studies look at the impact of 20–40 minutes of practice over a couple of months, and this is normally found to be plenty of time to see results.

The Conditions for Insight

It was some time ago, at the start of Chapter 7, that I first posed the question of how we can deliberately learn to be more creative, having shown that this form of decision making has been becoming increasingly important and that this trend can only be expected to continue. Since then we have been on a wide-ranging exploration of many aspects of what it takes to develop a creative decision-making capability that we can trust, encompassing:

- the qualities of mindset required for creativity: tenacity, openness and insight
- the requirement for balance between our instinctive, emotional, intellectual and intuitive mental capabilities
- the need to approach this kind of personal development from the inside out
- the huge possibility for change enabled by our brain's natural neuroplasticity
- the power of attention, provided it is done consciously and deliberately
- the three principles for success in addressing adaptive challenges
- the critical importance of our position on the reaction–response continuum
- why stress is so debilitating and damaging to performance
- the characteristics of the optimal performance state
- the significance of the seesaw-like operation of the frontal lobe and amygdala
- how we can literally rewire our brain to be less fearful
- the role of mindfulness and meditation in developing intentional attention
- how to limit the problems created by the boundaries to our awareness.

I've done my best to point you towards a solution for each of these challenges and opportunities, except one: how we can become more insightful? The question remains, is there anything that we can deliberately do to improve the intuitive faculty of our mind and brain? Many people instinctively answer "no" to this question, but science says otherwise, and once again a powerful key is meditation.

The form of meditation that I've spent the most time practising is one of the oldest, dating back over 2,500 years, to the time of the Buddha, known as Vipassana meditation. Vipassana is a Pali word, and it is most commonly translated as "insight"! The name recognises what has been learnt by experience: that this approach offers a process of ever-increasing awareness, where progress in understanding occurs as a series of step-changes, i.e. leaps of insight, rather than in a linear way.

There's a simple reason why Vipassana has survived for all this time: it has been proven beyond doubt that it changes people in a predictable and positive way. If you'd like to see an example of its effectiveness in the most challenging of circumstances, I recommend watching the short documentary "Doing Time Doing Vipassana", which follows the impact of a Vipassana meditation programme on the inmates in an Indian jail.

Given the scientifically validated understanding that neuro-science now provides about how meditation changes the brain, perhaps this outcome seems less surprising than it might have done when the film was made. However, for most people, I suspect the idea that we can experience a real internal shift simply by closing our eyes and focusing on the breath, would seem fanciful. Nevertheless, it works, and it does so because it dampens our sense of danger so that the world literally becomes less hostile for us. It turns out that this helps a lot with insight as well (Big Question 7).

The nature of insights is that the experience of them is usually sudden and unexpected – the familiar aha! moment – which makes them seem difficult to explain, much less consciously create. However, when people are connected to an electroencephalogram (EEG) recording brain activity, scientists can predict who will have an insight experience before it happens because the brain shows very consistent indicators:

- It is always relaxed yet focused, which is evidenced by synchronised brain waves at a much slower frequency than those which would normally dominate when we are awake and focused on specific tasks.
- There will be a burst of very high frequency brain waves, known as gamma waves, approximately 0.3 seconds before conscious awareness of the insight.

This may not be all that surprising either, because in the last chapter, when we looked at the mental state that exists when you get your creative ideas, I made the bet that you would be relaxed at the time. It was a confident bet, because it was backed up by neuroscience. I also highlighted the finding that creative people use their brains in a particular way – one that has more in common with dreaming than thinking. By taking a different look at brain activity, I can now explain why I said that.

Our brain always has some electrical activity going on, and here too, as with other brain functions, we need balance between the different frequencies. However, one will tend to be dominant, which is recognised as the current brain state. These brainwaves are grouped into five types according to frequency:

Gamma waves, measured in brainwave cycles per second (Hz) from 40 Hz up to around 200 Hz, are involved in higher processing tasks associated with perception and consciousness. Gamma waves don't exist on their own (there is no gamma state of mind), always being present with the other types, and are thought to be important to learning, memory and the synthesis of information from different parts of the brain.

Beta waves, operating at 13–40 Hz, occur in our normal waking state. They happen when we are thinking in a conscious way, such as completing goal-oriented tasks.

Alpha waves, in the range 9–12 Hz, are present when we are relaxed; we'll go into alpha, for example, as we start to drift off to sleep.

Theta waves are 4–8 Hz, and normally occur during light sleep or extreme relaxation.

Delta waves, which are 0.1–3 Hz, occur during deep, dreamless sleep.

So, we spend most of our thinking time in beta waves, at times relaxing into alpha or even theta. To slightly overgeneralise, *slower* here is *better*. Too much beta activity (especially at the high end of the range) is associated with stress, while the right amount aids focus. Stress also causes the brain to go out of synchronisation. Alpha waves, meanwhile, are associated with a better ability to recall memories, less discomfort and pain, reduced stress, and the harmonisation of brain waves. The alpha state is also associated with peak performance – people in "flow" have reduced beta brainwave activity.

When our brain is operating at theta frequencies, it creates a highly receptive mental state, as demonstrated by hypnotherapy, because it gives much greater access to our subconscious. Theta helps improve both intuition and creativity, and creative people are able to experience these brainwaves to a significantly greater extent than what we might call "normal" people. Delta further magnifies this effect, allowing connection to the deepest level of the unconscious.

One of the very clear effects of meditation is to slow down the dominant frequency of the brain and to synchronise brainwaves. The fact that stress is associated with high beta activity may help to explain why brainwave frequencies slow down with meditation.

If you think back to the neural seesaw that I explained in the last chapter, when we focus attention internally, the mind gets the message that we are safe, so the fight-or-flight mechanism tunes down. This can be seen from the reduction of both activity and grey matter in the amygdala.

How quickly can we expect these benefits? Even relative beginners have been found to be able to create an increase in alpha rhythms, while more experienced meditators can easily access theta, and even delta. Gamma activity is also believed to be closely related to expert levels of meditation practice.

Overall then, by practising meditation, without really "doing" anything, you will create the conditions for insight – a brain state that combines the slow, synchronised brainwaves found in alpha and theta, with the gamma activity that precedes aha! moments. You will then have conditioned yourself to be more creative.

Decision-Making Principle #10
Learning to pay deliberate attention may be the most valuable skill we can develop, because it underpins and maximises not just our capacity for creative decision making, but also any other form of adaptive learning.

Notes

1. Timothy D. Wilson et al., "Just think: The challenges of the disengaged mind" (2014) *Science*, 345(6192): 75.
2. Ben Evans, "Missed warnings: The fatal flaws which doomed challenger", *Space Safety Magazine*, www.spacesafetymagazine.com/space-disasters/challenger-disaster/missed-warnings-fatal-flaws-doomed-challenger.

3. H. A. Slagter, A. Lutz, L. L. Greischar, A. D. Francis, S. Nieuwenhuis, J. M. Davis et al., "Mental training affects distribution of limited brain resources" (2007) *PLoS Biology*, 5(6): e138.

4. Yi-Yuan Tang et al., "Short-term meditation training improves attention and self-regulation", (2007) *Proceedings of the National Academy of Sciences of the United States of America*, 104(43): 17152–17156.

CONCLUSION

"What is the secret of success?
Right decisions.
How do you make right decisions?
Experience.
How do you gain experience?
Wrong decisions."

—A. P. J. Abdul Kalam
(former President of India)

There is clearly some truth in the short dialogue above; indeed, I opened this book with a statement very like its first two lines, when I said that the quality of our decisions determines how well every other talent or capability that we have can be applied. That said, I find myself dissatisfied with the apparent finality of the conclusion that we can only improve our decisions through the experience of making mistakes. Ever since I started putting together my first workshop on the subject, I've been wondering how far we could progress in improving our decision making, and to what degree we can do so without the errors.

In this search, I've read countless books and articles, including the one I consider to be the best book on decision-making biases that I've found, *Thinking, Fast and Slow*, by Daniel Kahneman, which summarises his decades of research on the subject. He is a widely recognised expert, having been awarded the Nobel Prize, and this book won the 2012 National Academies Communication Award as the best creative work that helps people to understand scientific, engineering or medical subjects. Part of the reason that I avoided spending much time on decision-making biases in this book was because I couldn't see how to add further value in this area, with Kahneman (and many others) having written so extensively on the subject. Yet, perhaps ironically, it was a comment by Kahneman himself, in his conclusion to *Thinking, Fast and Slow*, that has probably prompted me to think about the challenge of reducing decision-making errors more than any other single thing. In response to questions that he poses himself – "what can be done about biases?" and "how can we improve judgments and decisions?" – he wrote:

> *"The short answer is that little can be achieved without a considerable investment of effort … Except for some effects that I attribute mostly to age, my intuitive thinking is just as prone to … [various biases] … as it was before I made a study of these issues."*

How can it be that one of the world's leading experts on the subject, who has studied it for decades and clearly understands it incredibly well, feels that all his effort has barely improved his intuitive judgment? If he is right, then the opening quote from A.P.J. Abdul Kalam might actually be overly optimistic, because Daniel Kahneman seems to suggest that even the experience of making the wrong decisions doesn't naturally lead to a significantly higher likelihood of making the right decisions the next time.

In contrast, by the time I'd finished my engineering degree, I knew that I had a very well-developed intuitive feeling for whether the answers to complex calculations were about right; we all had to develop this capability to reduce the risk that just one data entry error on our calculator could result in a huge miscalculation by the end of the problem. We had simply given regular attention to the task, for long enough, with feedback, and had become good at it. In the same way, top golfers don't hit the ball with their conscious mind, though they start off learning what to do that way. Then, by focusing attention on practising doing what they know over and over, the subconscious mind learns to take over. If it didn't, they would never hit the ball well.

Furthermore, because of the neuroplasticity of the brain, it is unsurprising that this process has been found to be the basis of development of any skill. Experts in every field become that way through intentional practice, not ageing! In extreme cases, like the aircraft spotters in Chapter 1, or when we learned to ride a bike, the conscious mind doesn't even have to understand what to do in the first place – demonstrating that when the subconscious does anything repetitively, and gets feedback, that focus of attention leads to learning.

The foundational role of attention, without which learning doesn't take place, is why I have suggested that the ability to focus attention with intention is the ultimate skill.

The Need for Mindful Awareness

I can see no logical reason why decision making would be exempt from this principle – why would conditioning not apply here? This apparent anomaly needs explanation. What is the missing piece? Given that expertise requires unconscious competence, it seemed to me that the problem must originate from an error in one of two assumptions:

- That the conscious mind can be trained to better recognise, and thereby to correct, unconscious errors.
- That studying and understanding, at a conscious level, the nature of unconscious biases, would (somehow) lead to a reduction in the occurrence of those biases.

The first of these possibilities is easy to exclude, if we consider it only at face value; research highlights that we can quickly learn to recognise the type of situations where errors are likely. For example, as we saw in Chapter 1, once you are aware of hindsight bias, it is relatively simple to pause after an event where something went wrong, to remind yourself that what seems totally apparent now might not have been nearly so black and white at the time. We know that after the event, it tends to be obvious what the critical factor that was overlooked was, which makes it feel as though it should have been equally unmissable at the time of the decision. But, with awareness, it is relatively easy to see that, before the outcome was known, there were also 20 other equally likely outcomes, with no practical way to differentiate between them. As such, awareness can protect us against the error.

As you saw in the last chapter and elsewhere, however, the deeper level of truth is that it can be very hard to notice anything the mind is not looking for (remember my dad's bike in Chapter 10?). So, turning awareness of our hindsight bias into a practical reality requires considerable alertness – or present moment awareness – before there is any chance we'll consistently notice those times when the bias could be a problem. I might know that ice on the road makes driving dangerous, but if I can't spot the ice, that awareness is essentially useless. Training to overcome hindsight bias, or any other unconscious source of mental errors, needs to extend beyond understanding to also include mindful awareness, or mindfulness.

In the case of the second bullet, the problem is less obvious. There is clearly something important going on if Daniel Kahneman's enormous expertise and knowledge doesn't readily convert into improved judgment. My belief is that this can be explained through our understanding of technical and adaptive learning. The conscious and subconscious minds process the world very differently, and I explained in Chapter 8 why the technical, skill-based learning that resulted from his research will not naturally lead to the adaptive learning necessary to create unconscious change. Hence, perhaps it is not surprising that he expressed the belief that, "little can be achieved without a considerable investment of effort" – because it seems that his practice was not directed effectively at the necessary part of the brain. It would be easy to believe that learning to hit a tennis ball well is very difficult if all you ever practised was a badminton swing.

"Get into the Water"

Studies these days are indicating that remarkably little of the right type of practice can make a significant difference. One such study assessed the application of mindfulness in leadership;[1] those who practised for as little as 10 minutes per day were found to "progress significantly more" than those who did not. Furthermore, as would be expected due to this change being adaptive in nature, researchers found that those who only attended the workshops, but then did not practise, did not improve; while for the others, more was better.

Once we know that the brain is much like the body, responding by becoming better developed in any area where we challenge it, this finding is completely unsurprising, isn't it? As I've said in a similar way before, we wouldn't expect that being taught how to use a weights machine to build a muscle would benefit us, unless we sat down and pushed weights!

Thus, by taking a mindfulness-based approach to improving decision making, it is clear that we can be quite a bit more optimistic about the possibility that we might be able to make more "right decisions" than indicated in the opening quote. Once we fully understand how inner transformation can lead to changes in the external environment, as discussed in Chapter 5, it is easy to see that there are many times when it should be possible to shift our external results without having to make bad decisions first, enabled by an inner transformation that reduces the impact of our decision-making biases. But if you really want to know what I'm talking about, you'll need to experience the benefits for yourself, and that means you are going to have to start to practise. We can't learn to swim, or even know what it really means to swim, unless we get into the water.

In this book on decision making, I have built a case for the vital importance of mindfulness, and introduced you to the most basic principles for practising it. For more depth, there is already a plethora of books and apps that can help you in this area. For newcomers especially, but also for more experienced practitioners, *Mindfulness in Plain English*, by Bhante Henepola Gunaratana, provides an excellent starting point, because it is comprehensive, simply presented, and has a brilliant section on overcoming some of the common problems that people experience which can easily lead to unnecessary frustration, even to them giving up.

I'm not asking you to trust me that this investment of your time will be worth it. I'm suggesting that you trust the neuroscientists who have been demonstrating for decades that meditation changes the brain in beneficial ways. That said, I can tell you that I've done my own EEG test, so that I could look at my brain before and after meditation, and also after a concentrated period of practice. The changes were remarkable, showing both a dramatic slowing of my brainwaves and all the parts of my brain becoming better balanced and integrated. It left me in no doubt of the effectiveness of this approach to changing mindset.

Transformation via the Ten Principles

One of the great things about science is that it is always advancing. The progress of the last few decades has enabled an exploration of the brain that has clearly demonstrated the power of mindful awareness to improve decision making. Neuroscientists have literally been able to observe deliberately created changes taking place at the level of the wiring in the brain. Although scientific understanding in this area will no doubt continue to grow, it seems unlikely that these basic findings will be disproven – now that it has been established that the world is not flat, it will never be flat again, and now we know that the brain is neuroplastic, surely the same must be true. So, logically, I hope the power of mindful attention makes sense to you.

In this book, I've also tried to explain why we appear to be so irrational at times, showing how our behaviours make sense once we understand the priorities of the instinctive and emotional brains. I have tried to create both a logical and emotional connection to a set of fundamental ideas that can weaken the negative influences of these unconscious drivers, replacing them with more automatically positive choices instead. Most of the ten principles I've introduced are powerful on their own, but together they become so much more so. Viewed together, I hope their synergy is evident, producing a formula for the deliberate development and application of your conscious mind in such a way that it can confidently be relied upon to enable a radical shift of mindset and a positive transformation in your decision making.

No Place for Old Dogs – New Tricks Required

1. We can access much more of our potential by learning to harness, in a deliberate way, the power of our unconscious mind.

2. A prerequisite of making progress is that we leave the known behind, being willing to break some established "rules" about the way things happen.

3. As the pace of change increases, we'll face more and more "unknown unknowns", and that will place a new emphasis on the need for creativity in forward planning.

Mindset Matters! – Getting Beyond the Process

4. We have an extraordinary level of ability to convince ourselves that we are right, and to ignore contradictory evidence – even when we are profoundly wrong.

5. It is impossible to experience "reality", or to be "objective", because everything is processed unconsciously prior to awareness. By shifting our perception of "reality", we will automatically start to make new choices.

6. Stress drives maladaptive choices and decisions, so the reduction of stress will tend to improve decision making.

7. Making decisions creatively, rather than by using a problem-solving approach, requires us to use our mind differently, learning to apply the conscious mind to the task of balancing and regulating the brain so that its different parts operate together more effectively. The key qualities of mind required are tenacity, openness and insightfulness.

Transforming Decision Making from the Inside Out

8. Developing the mind is an inside-out challenge, necessitating that we harness the neuroplastic nature of the brain by learning to focus attention with intention.

9. As we practise intentional attention, we can predictably and reliably evolve our brain to reduce reactivity and become more responsive, flexible and adaptive.

10. Learning to pay deliberate attention may be the most valuable skill we can develop, because it underpins and maximises not just our capacity for creative decision making, but also any other form of adaptive learning.

As I have been writing, I have been regularly confronted with the reality of something that Mark Twain said: "A successful book is not made of what is in it, but of what is left out of it." For example, there is much evidence that a *positive* mindset is vital to good decision making. I could easily have devoted a whole chapter to this topic, but in the balance, I felt that by dealing with stress the same fundamental aspects of mindset can be produced, and that therefore other factors would make a more valuable contribution in the space available.

We could also have discussed things like group decision making, social factors to do with how we relate to others, the impact of physical aspects such as diet, exercise and sleep, ethical questions and how the adult mind develops. Each is important, and deeper awareness would be helpful. However, just as we saw with Daniel Kahneman's experience of putting his own research into practice, most of them would be difficult to integrate without first being able to reduce reactivity and increase responsiveness. As I hope I've demonstrated, until that has been achieved, your decision making will let you down just when you need it the most – when you are under stress – therefore, helping you with the achievement of that goal was my top priority.

Figure C.1 contrasts the mindfully responsive state that can be realised with practice, as you learn to master the ten principles, with the relatively mindless default mode that is so automatic for so many people so much of the time.

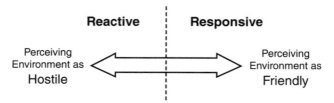

Reactive	Responsive

Perceiving Environment as **Hostile** ←——————→ Perceiving Environment as **Friendly**

Mindless:
- Easily distracted
- Stressed
- Closed – habits dominate
- Disengaged
- Externally motivated
- Outside-in attention

Mindful:
- Clarity of focus
- Relaxed
- Open – pot'l for creativity
- Absorbed/in "flow"
- Internally motivated
- Inside-out attention

Figure C.1

The transformation in decision making that results as mindfulness increases can be trusted, because it is a natural consequence of a shift in perception of the environment, away from the feeling that we must protect ourselves, which introduces stress, and towards relaxation-inducing safety. It is inevitable, because it is the result of the frontal lobe becoming more active and the amygdala quietening down, which creates the specific benefits to creative decision making of increasing openness and insightfulness. Once we've learnt to use it effectively, the conscious capacity of the higher brain enables us to detach from our instincts, emotions and conditioned behaviours, so that we can move from reaction to response. This involves a shift away from the *outside-in* variety of attention used by our survival mechanism and heuristics, where our focus gets dragged in the direction of whatever most interests, or frightens, the unconscious mind. Its place is taken by the mindful cultivation of the slower, more conscious, *inside-out* form of attention that I've described.

The benefits of conditioning yourself to manage reactivity in this way will only increase as the environment continues to evolve, becoming more complex and fast moving. Paradoxically, perhaps, as things on the outside speed up, and the number of distractions increase, it becomes more important that we learn to slow down. This is a mindset, not a skillset. Your starting point is simply a decision to cooperate with the process by practising becoming more intentional about the way you use your conscious capabilities. I wish you great speed on your journey.

Note

1. Megan Reitz and Michael Chaskalson, "Mindfulness works but only if you work at it", *Harvard Business Review*, 4 November 2016.

INDEX